Who Is My
Enemy?

Who Is My Enemy?

Questions
American Christians Must Face
about Islam—and Themselves

Lee C. Camp

BrazosPress

a division of Baker Publishing Group
Grand Rapids, Michigan

© 2011 by Lee C. Camp

Published by Brazos Press
a division of Baker Publishing Group
P.O. Box 6287, Grand Rapids, MI 49516-6287
www.brazospress.com

Printed in the United States of America

Library of Congress Cataloging-in-Publication Data

Camp, Lee C.
    Who is my enemy? : questions American Christians must face about Islam—and themselves / Lee C. Camp.
        p.   cm.
    Includes bibliographical references (p.   ) and index.
    ISBN 978-1-58743-288-0 (pbk.)
    1. Islam—United States. 2 Christianity—United States. 3. Islam—Relations—Christianity. 4. Christianity and other religions—Islam. 5. Ethnic conflict—Religious aspects. 6. Violence—Religious aspects—Islam. 7. Violence—Religious aspects—Christianity. 8. Political messianism—United States. I. Title.
BP67.U6C36 2011
261.2′97—dc22   2011015452

Published in association with the literary agency of Daniel Literary Group, LLC, Nashville, TN.

11   12   13   14   15   16   17   7   6   5   4   3   2   1

To my parents

You've heard it said, "Love your neighbor and hate your enemy." But I say, Love your enemies and pray for those who persecute you, so you may be children of your Father in heaven; for God makes the sun to rise on both the evil and the good, and sends rain on both the righteous and the unrighteous. If you love those who love you—well, so what? Even mobsters love that way, don't they? And if you show care only to your brothers and sisters—well, what's the big deal there? Even those who have no relation with God love that way, don't they? So, grow up—into the sort of whole and complete love with which your heavenly Father loves.

—Matthew 5:43–48 (author's translation)

Our struggle is not against enemies of flesh and blood, but against the rulers, authorities, and cosmic powers of this present darkness.

—Ephesians 6:12 (author's translation)

Contents

Preface

"Public Enemy Number One" was killed last night.

The night before I signed off on the proofs of this book, Osama bin Laden was killed. The United States' Public Enemy Number One for a decade and the mastermind of the 9/11 terrorist plots, bin Laden had been hunted down and his death was greeted with widespread revelry and celebration. The media reported student gatherings in front of the White House complete with chants of "U-S-A!" President Obama, in announcing the killing of bin Laden, asserted, "Justice has been done." Numerous government officials called bin Laden's death a "victory against terrorism."

But how do we determine *who* our enemies are? *And*, who is the *we*? "Our enemies are not flesh and blood," said the apostle Paul. Nonetheless, if we do identify "enemy" with any given person, how can killing that enemy be a victory for those who follow the Jesus who taught us to love our enemies? Moreover, does our celebration of such killing really serve as a victory over the forces of terror? Certainly Osama bin Laden, his body cast into the sea, will himself foment no more terror and strife. But ultimately, can such vengeance overcome evil? Can there even be such a thing as a "war against terror"? If the light of Christ has overcome the darkness through suffering love, if at the cross of Christ the justice of God was satisfied, and if we are called to take up our cross and follow Jesus, what then? Could it be that the killing of Osama bin Laden is but a continuation of bin

Laden's ways, which in the end can only be overcome in the long-suffering love of Christ?

These are neither trivial nor flippant questions, and I raise them with much trepidation.

A few months ago I sat across the table from a man who had been described by the local media as stirring up the populace by warning of a coming Muslim threat to America.[1] Knowing that theology is biographically informed, I began by asking him to tell me his story of what brought him to the questions and concerns that were animating him in recent years. He told of being raised a conservative southern Christian, later becoming an Episcopalian, and still later a serious Buddhist. But after September 11, 2001, he recounted, he no longer had interest in Buddhism but would spend his time studying the Qur'an and the Sunna (the words and deeds of Muhammad).

He grabbed a piece of paper and, employing the handwriting of the scientist he is by training, recounted his statistical analysis of how often war-making is discussed in the texts of Islam,[2] the Old Testament, and the New Testament: 31 percent for the Islamic texts; 5.3 percent for the Old Testament; and 0 percent for the New Testament, he claimed.[3] We talked at great length about his understanding of the texts. He clearly believes Islam to be a threat, and dangerous. I recounted alternate interpretations, citing a prominent Muslim theologian in Jerusalem. He responded by saying he cares nothing about "Muslimology." "I don't care what any Muslim may *say* about the Qur'an or Islam; I only care about the authoritative original *texts*," he said in effect.

It just so happened that we were two doors down from the mosque on Twelfth Avenue in Nashville. About that time a young man entered the shop, who, from the looks of his apparel, was Muslim. So I said to the man across the table from me, "Have you ever met with local Muslims, talked to them any?"

"No."

"Why not?"

"Because Muhammad teaches them that I am their enemy. So if they are Muslims, I am by definition their enemy. And since they believe that Muhammad was one of the greatest of men, I cannot be friends with someone like that. They are my enemy."

I share with you in this book my own recent journey, trying to make sense of such claims. What are we to make of the apparent threat posed by Muslim militants, and what are we to make of the perceived differences between Christianity and Islam? I have come to think there are some things that need to be said that are not being said, so I started digging around, traveling where I could, and having conversations with folks I never dreamed of having conversations with, in order to better say these things. This journey has taken me not only to the mosque in Nashville but also to the Blue Mosque in Istanbul; to the Oklahoma City National Memorial, where an angry American ex-military man killed 168 people in cold blood; to Hebron, where I would drink Coke with a lifelong PLO activist and colleague of Arafat; to the hills above the Sea of Galilee, where I would read the Sermon on the Mount; to the Old City of Jerusalem, where the blood of Muslims ran deep at the hands of Christian Crusaders; and to New York City and Ground Zero, where the blood of many tribes and tongues was spilled at the hands of Muslim militants.

In this process I have found myself rattled again by what Jesus actually taught and lived, and I frankly wish sometimes that he had taught and said something different than he did. And I have discovered tales and truths both troubling and challenging, which I share herein.[4]

Book writing, like any good work, demonstrates that our myths about individualism are untrue. All work worth doing is necessarily dependent upon the work, goodwill, support, and kindnesses of others. I am thankful for Lipscomb University, the daily Christian community of which I am grateful to be a part, especially Provost Craig Bledsoe for research funding; Craig Katzenmiller and Jonathan Melton, former students and now friends who provided research assistance on this project; the support of the staff of Beaman Library, especially Carolyn Wilson and Rachel Pyle; my dean, Professor Terry Briley, my departmental chair, George Goldman, and all my colleagues in the College of Bible and Ministry and the Hazelip School of Theology, with whom I share a Christian community in which much is held dearly in common, while enough is not held in common to provide us sufficient opportunity to practice charity one with the other, and they most often with me; and Randy Lowry, president of Lipscomb University, who continues to challenge us all to do good work well.

I count it a great gift to have been called to the vocation of teaching. I thank my many students who have paid attention to the questions we raise together, who have never let me utter glib platitudes without asking how the gospel must be embodied in real life, and how it is embodied in my own life.

Special thanks to the Louisville Institute, under the direction of James Lewis, whose Christian Faith and Life Grant accorded opportunity for writing and research, as well as travel to the Middle East. In Palestine, I was very graciously and kindly received by the staff at Tantur Ecumenical Institute. There, Fr. Michael McGarry Sr., Bridget Tighe, and all the staff and scholars in residence received me with great hospitality, and I thank them for allowing me space and time and support for my first stay in that land. Professor Mustafa Abu Sway and Fr. David Burrell were especially gracious to me and of great encouragement. In Istanbul, I was also graciously received by the faculty at Fatih University. This work would not have been possible without such support and would certainly not be very interesting without such engaging and lively conversation.

I also thank the following individuals who read all or portions of the manuscript and gave such gracious, helpful, and challenging feedback: David Burrell, Jim and Gayle Camp, Everett Ferguson, David Fleer, Josh Graves, Gyasi McKenzie, Scot McKnight, Melissa Snarr, Glen Stassen, Mustafa Abu Sway, Ken Switzer, and Marshall Switzer. Greg Daniel, author-agent extraordinaire, helped envision this work, and Rodney Clapp, wise counselor and gentle editor, has brought this project to reality. I thank them both, along with Lisa Ann Cockrel, BJ Heyboer, Lisa Williams, and all the staff of Brazos Press. I also thank the many fellow travelers at the Otter Creek Church who sustain, encourage, and challenge me.

I am profoundly grateful for my wife, Laura, and for the relationship God has given us. We have shared so many wonderful times and difficult times together, and I give great thanks. And to be the father of three sons—Chandler, David, and Benjamin—what great joy, a blessing beyond measure. Finally, I dedicate this book to my parents, Jim and Gayle Camp, who first called me to seek first the kingdom of God.

I thank all these, without assuming that any of them agree with the contents herein. Some of them, no doubt, disagree on important points. Moreover, there is so much more that needs to be said; but book writing is like picture painting in this regard: it can never be done, never perfected. One must simply find a good stopping place, and I pray that I have chosen such a place to stop working on this particular project.

1

The Muslim Enemy

... all these people who want to kill us ...
—A Nashville resident,
on the local Muslim population

On a recent Independence Day, I delivered a lecture in which I shared my developing understanding of Christian and Muslim views of war and peacemaking. In the question-and-answer period that followed, a woman noted that since it was the Fourth of July, we should all be very thankful for our liberties. That being the case, she asked, how should we respond to those people just down the street here in Nashville, down at the mosque on Twelfth Avenue, "all these people who want to kill us?"

I was so taken aback, I found it difficult to know how to respond to the cavalier stereotyping of one and a half billion people. "I don't think the people on Twelfth Avenue do want to kill us," I said after a moment of awkward silence. "I do," she responded without pause. "Why . . . well . . . ," I stammered, "have you talked to any of the people on Twelfth Avenue?" "No," she replied, "but I've read books." I was sure—and I said so—that she was quite terribly wrong. But I

1

was not equipped sufficiently, either intellectually or experientially, to articulate all the ways in which she was wrong. Nor was I sufficiently equipped to voice my conviction that her companion was also wrong. He had raised an objection that I had previously heard from others, that there is only one way to understand the Muslim's view of the world: there is the house of Islam and the house of war. Those not submitted to Islam must be the target of war until they submit. And moreover, he said, any Muslim who says otherwise is merely practicing the Islamic art of deceit. When I cited one source from a well-credentialed Muslim scholar to the contrary, the man replied, "I don't care what your little book says. I'm telling the truth."

I was already acquainted with such hostility. One pleasant November morning I strolled to the end of our driveway to peruse the morning paper before leaving for the ivory tower where I hang my shingle. Reading the Nashville morning paper is no habit of mine. Pure self-interest motivated me, expecting a story to mention a lecture I had delivered at an "interfaith gathering." Our university's new Institute for Conflict Management convened the gathering to make space for honest dialogue among practitioners of various faiths in Nashville. As a faculty member of the university, I was assigned to speak on the "Theological Ground for Peaceful Coexistence."

In the Southeast, where our particular Christian tradition has its largest number of congregations in the United States, it has not been uncommon for jokes to be made regarding our sense of superiority, our historical sense that we have been the only "real" Christians, that we embody the "true church," and no others. The stereotype is in many ways out-of-date, but stereotypes die a slow death. Thus, for us to host a gathering of not merely different sorts of Christians but also adherents of other religions was no small step. It had been, I thought, a good day. I was impressed that there was none of the drivel that seems often to pervade ecumenical or interreligious sorts of talk, none of that pabulum that suggests we are "all saying the same thing, just in different ways."

But serious conversations, carefully nuanced and peppered with rhetorical questions, can quickly get misconstrued. The story I expected to be buried deep in "Local News" was instead an above-the-fold front-page story titled "Christians Must 'Let Go' of Some Beliefs for Sake of Peace, Theologian Says." Readers concluded I had argued that we should "let go" of the lordship of Jesus precisely for such so-called peace.[1] I uttered an expletive and went into the house to let my wife know it was going to be a long day.

When I arrived at my office shortly thereafter, I was dismayed when one of the departmental assistants knocked on my door to let me know that a Nashville talk-radio program was on the line, asking for me. In less than three hours, I had been contacted by talk radio in Detroit and Fox News in New York City and was getting unhappy emails from across the Southeast. The local Nashville rap station, one student reported to me later, held a call-in survey. I was found to be "stupid" by a wide margin. My inbox filled; the phone rang incessantly—hundreds of messages by the end of the day. I heard from people across Tennessee, then California, New Zealand, Manhattan, and Israel. By the end of the day, I had been called a moron, an idiot, a *dhimmi*, and an a**hole. The following evening's lead news story on the local Fox affiliate covered the uproar, complete with name-calling and demands that my job be revoked without further delay.

If the task of a theologian is to stir people up, one colleague emailed me to say, you have had great success today.

A man wrote from Knoxville: "We need to broaden our belief's [*sic*] by giving up what we believe? You're worse than an idiot because an idiot never knew. You're simply an a**hole." An old college classmate wrote to tell me that I had become "a joke to common sense, decency, and intelligence." Those who believed themselves to understand Islam—especially a number of people apparently spurred to polemical action because of a posting on an apparently right-wing political blog[2]—wrote to chastise my lack of understanding of Islam. The subject line of one email—"Professor Dhimmi"—caught my attention. I did not yet know what a "dhimmi" was.

> I read that you are teaching your students that they must renounce some of their Christian values if they want to live in peace with Islam. Where did you get that idea? Do you truly understand what Islam teaches? The Umma views the world in 2 parts; the house of Islam and the house of war. There can never be peace until there is just the house of Islam. Non Muslims are given 3 choices per the

Qur'an; convert, submit or accept dhimmitude, or die. Then there will be peace.

Many wrote to say similar things. There can be no peace. Muslims do not want peace. They want you to convert, or they will kill you, and if they say otherwise, then they are lying.

The respondents seemed to fall into two camps. There were those who incorrectly concluded that I had publicly denied the faith, that I had publicly professed that we should "let go" of the lordship of Jesus in order to get along with Jews and Muslims. Some of these respondents, though deeply troubled, were nonetheless gracious in their response. An email from New Zealand (!) received late in the day admonished me with the words of the apostle Paul: "I marvel that you are turning away so soon from Him who called you in the grace of Christ, to a different gospel."

But there was another group whose starting point was simply fear. Some of them were (and some were not) interested in Christian orthodoxy. But they were clearly fearful of Muslims. My lecture had indeed suggested that the church must "let go" of an attempt to dominate the world, must "let go" of medieval Christendom models that continue to live on in contemporary American Christian communities. This struck a vein of fear: there can be no dialogue with Muslims, no parley with the enemy, no trusting conversation, because the enemy simply wants to convert you, kill you, or make you submit.

So another email, apparently from a real estate developer in Memphis, came with the subject line "Professor Dhimmi is your name." *Dhimmi*—a new vocabulary word twice in one day. *Dhimmi* is not in the Webster's dictionary I have on my shelf. Several of my colleagues did not know the word either. I would learn that a *dhimmi* is a poll tax paid to Muslim authorities in exchange for protection, typically required from Jews and Christians. The developer said:

> I will not give up my belief that Jesus Christ is the son of God and that he is Lord of all—period. I believe there are several hundred million other Christians who believe the same way and are willing to die to defend their beliefs. There will be no peace with Muslims because that is not what they want. Muslims want one of three things—converts, dhimmis, or death.

4

By the way—the Crusades were the Christian response to Muslims raping, pillage, and killing everyone in their path that stood up to them as they swept across Europe. Learn some history you moron.

I actually *would* learn more about the Crusades, and I would learn that the one who called me a moron (in Jesus's name, of course) actually knew less about the Crusades than he apparently thought.

But that would be later. At the time, I found that day's events instructive for my own inner life. I realized the immense power of media and the rapid ease with which media can misconstrue substantive conversations. I realized, in later reflection, how vain and fearful I am. My own university and church community were immensely supportive, but I realized that I nonetheless remain a people-pleaser. I still want everyone to like me. More perniciously, I realized how much I like attention: "All press is good press," someone told me, and there was a deep place that resonated with the attention, a realization that prompted shame. I would confess later to a mentor that the greedy part of me was pleased with the thought that the attention might mean I sell more books. And, on the other hand, I realized how one's own psyche, when publicly called names and made a public spectacle, if only for one's fifteen minutes of infamy, leads one to duck one's head and keep quiet so as not to be dubbed a troublemaker.

There also remained this nagging question: what *do* I really know about Islam? The furor, the fear, the outright hostility—what was behind this? Had I been a dupe? (One emailer compared my reconciling words to the acts of Neville Chamberlain.) Moreover, why had I, as a faculty member in a university with explicit Christian commitments, never taken time to have any substantive conversations with Muslims, especially when a mosque sits just about a mile north of our campus? I realized my own failing to get to know my neighbors. And thus some new experiences began to unfold.

2

To Seek to Understand Rather Than to Be Understood

Eight or nine years ago, I was frustrated with some new policy at our university, and I turned to one of my colleagues after a faculty meeting and said, "That really makes me mad." He looked at me, laughed, and replied, "You're always mad." It was a stinging, revelatory moment for me. Something of an addiction to the rush of the state of being offended had developed.

About that time in my life I rediscovered the beautiful prayer traditionally attributed to Francis of Assisi:

> Lord, make us instruments of your peace. Where there is hatred, let us sow love; where there is injury, pardon; where there is discord, union; where there is doubt, faith; where there is despair, hope; where there is darkness, light; where there is sadness, joy. Grant that we may not so much seek to be consoled as to console; to be understood as to understand; to be loved as to love. For it is in giving that we receive; it is in pardoning that we are pardoned; and it is in dying that we are born to eternal life. *Amen.*[1]

"Double Vision"

To seek to understand rather than first to be understood; rather than indulging my anger and the desire to be offended, I first listen well to the other. What if we were to take this approach as a theological method? That is, rather than a posture of fear, condemnation, or resentment, what would it mean to employ what Alan Jacobs calls a "hermeneutic of love"?[2] What would it mean to seek to read texts and engage in theological conversation with no other goal than to love God and neighbor and enemy? Miroslav Volf's excellent book *Exclusion and Embrace* employs different terminology but a similar approach, which he calls "double vision." He does not mean by this "fuzzy vision." Instead, he calls us to look at things from another perspective, namely, the perspective of our enemies. In doing so, we may be able to see things we could not possibly see otherwise:

> We enlarge our thinking by letting the voices and perspectives of others, especially those with whom we may be in conflict, resonate within ourselves, by allowing them to help us see them, as well as ourselves, from *their* perspective, and if needed, readjust our perspectives as we take into account their perspectives. Nothing can guarantee in advance that the perspectives will ultimately merge and agreement be reached. We may find that we must reject the perspective of the other.[3]

But such a practice may also allow us, he notes, to bring our different conceptions of justice alongside one another so that our different understandings enrich one another and perhaps even issue forth in unexpected forms of agreement.

This is no call to some intellectually lazy relativism. On the one hand, it is important for us to reject the modernist conceit that it is possible to "see things as they really are," to see, as it were, with God's eyes. But to reject such an intellectual arrogance—that we can simply see things with timeless, universal eyes—is not the same thing as saying that one opinion is as good as any other.[4] But it is a call to intellectual humility. We are all finite human beings, belabored not only with our finitude but also with prejudices and presuppositions and our own experiences. That is, we all see things from our own perspective. All our knowing is "socially located." We see things as we see them, and at our best, we seek to describe the world as we see it and understand it, fairly and without self-promoting agendas, but all the while acknowledging that our seeing and knowing are inescapably mediated through our time, place, experience, and often, ill motives.[5]

Is there any theological ground for the practice of double vision, of seeking first to understand rather than to be understood? One obvious ground is found at the foot of the cross of Jesus. That is, whatever we learn or think we know must be mediated through what we first learn through a crucified Messiah. In my own experience, however, a theology of the cross is what very often drives the rhetoric of certainty and being offended. Someone might object, for example: "Does not Jesus's crucifixion presuppose that God is holy, that humankind is unholy, that God is a God of absolute righteousness who can hold no parley with unrighteousness? Playing intellectual games like double vision brings us nigh unto making a mockery of a crucified Lord, a Lord who died because of the wickedness and injustice of the unrighteous. Our task is not to try to understand the perspective of the wicked. Our task is to call them to repentance, to call them to embrace what we know is good and right."

But the manner of retelling the story of the crucifixion in Scripture invites us to see *ourselves* among the guilty perpetrators. "For us, sinful and limited human beings, following in the footsteps of the Crucified means not only creating space in ourselves for others, but . . . making also space for their perspective on us and on them."[6] If we take seriously the New Testament's insistence that we are all broken, all need a Great Physician, all are slaves to the "power of sin," then the principle of fallibility—that is, a deep awareness that I may be wrong and need to look for *my* part, for *our* part—inevitably follows.[7]

A second commitment that would lead us to the practice of double vision is simply the call to love our enemies. How can I possibly love one to whom I refuse to even listen? How can I possibly love one whose viewpoint or experience I refuse to grant even a hearing?

Double Vision at Ground Zero

My wife and I made our way to New York City on a recent September 11 to observe and pray. Saint Paul's Chapel sits just alongside the World Trade Center site and was a place of refuge for rescue workers and firefighters in the days of crisis surrounding the attacks. There I came across a small note, a thank-you note from a little girl for the tireless and self-sacrificing labor of the rescue workers and firefighters. She raised the question often heard in those days about the terrorist attackers: how could they do this to us? How could they do this?—this is an important question. But unfortunately this question often becomes dismissive rather than empathetic. What if we take that question as an authentic agenda of understanding? Really, how could our enemy see the world the way he or she does? What in their experience, in their presuppositions, in their vision, could contribute to the deeds or words or actions we find so unjust and horrid? And what might they see about us, from their perspective, that we might not see?

But the rhetoric we employ to express our outrage may shut ourselves off from the possibility of such questions. To call a certain number of nations the "axis of evil," for example, precludes asking such questions as these. No one wants to *talk to* or try to *understand* "evil." Moreover, even suggesting the practice of double vision might be construed as supporting evil. It should be obvious but must be said: this practice of self-examination in response to the evil done by another in no way removes accountability or responsibility for the wrongdoing of the other. This is not the point. Rather, the point is this: if we are even to begin to make space for the possibility of peacemaking or change, then we must first examine ourselves. This is, at one level, what Scripture means when it says, "Let judgment begin with the household of God," or when those in recovery speak of "keeping my side of the street clean."

Thus, double vision requires at least these two things: first, to see things as we see them, to do our best to articulate our understanding without apology or false humility, believing it to be genuinely true and not just "true for us." But second, believing as we do in enemy love, we seek to practice that enemy love through acts of empathy—an empathy that may not agree, approve, or necessarily even tolerate, but nonetheless seeks to understand. Some sort of practice like this, I suspect, is required to keep us from the bondage of bigotry. Perhaps for that reason alone, it is worth practicing. We may, in the process, learn more about ourselves than we learn about the one we call our enemy.

Double vision is one way of practicing common folk wisdom. "Don't criticize until you've walked a mile in the other person's shoes." But such wisdom requires a substantive level of moral maturity. It is a practice important not only in the moral growth of children, for example, but also in the character required to sustain marriages and other long-term relationships. If every argument is simply a resort to one spouse discussing the faults and failings of the other spouse, there can be little hope for reconciliation. A refusal to examine one's own failures—regardless of the wrong done by the other—is typically judged to be a basic character flaw. It seems to me that such a character flaw must be addressed if Christians are to get very far in seeking to understand Muslims. And vice versa.

"You Are Doing the Very Same Things"

Note too this more general biblical observation: the apostle Paul states that when one classifies oneself or one's own group as "righteous" and another as "unrighteous," one has thereby condemned oneself. In the first chapter of the letter to the Romans, Paul categorizes all sorts of wicked behavior. A reader might be whipped into a frenzy of self-righteous indignation reading Paul's catalog of indecencies and wickedness. And then the sting: "Therefore you have no excuse, whoever you are, when you judge others; for in passing judgment on another you condemn yourself, because you, the judge, are doing the very same things. You say, 'We know that God's judgment on those who do such things is in accordance with truth.' Do you imagine, whoever you are, that when you judge those who do such things and yet do them yourself, you will escape the judgment of God?" (Rom. 2:1–3).

"But we are *not* doing the 'very same things'! We haven't flown any airliners full of civilians into skyscrapers," someone might handily object. But the apostle's point is not that we share the same *symptoms* of "sin." One alcoholic may prefer cocktails, and another some Tennessee sipping whiskey. One shopping addict may prefer malls, and another the Home Shopping Network. One bigot may prefer white Americans, and another African Hutu. From Paul's perspective, one sinner may prefer lust, another greed, and another gossip. But it is all the same sickness.[8] To the degree that I eagerly catalog the sickness in another, says Paul's stinging indictment, to that degree do I condemn and judge myself.[9]

But even still, it is an undeniable historical fact that people who claim the lordship of Jesus—and to all appearances, claim the lordship of Jesus in a manner that they take quite seriously—have killed or participated in the killing of thousands and thousands of civilians in acts of horrid violence, certainly as horrid and malicious as the acts of September 11, 2001. Al Qaeda, may God have mercy, prefers airliners. They have done dastardly work. But the Pauline counsel would prompt us to remember other dastardly work and frightening words too, to remember that "our people," our Christian brothers and sisters have been caught up in similar dastardly work.

The most casual perusal of a classic work like Roland Bainton's *Christian Attitudes toward War and Peace* serves as the start of such an exercise: the call to war by Pope Urban II, the start of the Crusade to take Jerusalem from the Muslims, a war that employed "crucifixion, ripping open those who had swallowed coins, mutilation—Bohemond of Antioch sent to the Greek Emperor a whole cargo of noses and thumbs sliced from the Saracens." Regarding the capture of Jerusalem, Raymond of Aguilers recounted:

> Some of our men (and this was more merciful) cut off the heads of their enemies; others shot them with arrows, so that they fell from the towers; others tortured them longer by casting them into the flames. Piles of heads, hands, and feet were to be seen in the streets of the city. It was necessary to pick one's way over the bodies of men and horses. But these were small matters compared to what happened at the Temple of Solomon, a place where religious services are ordinarily chanted. What happened there? If I tell the truth, it will exceed your powers of belief. So let it suffice to say this much at least, that in the temple and portico of Solomon, men rode in blood up to their knees and the bridle reins. Indeed, it was a just and splendid judgment of God, that this place should be filled with the blood of the unbelievers, when it had suffered so long from their blasphemies.[10]

In the later so-called wars of religion—though we will ask whether this is a helpful designation—the Catholics sought to slay the Protestants in great number, and the Protestant Huguenots, for their part, "wore strings of priest's ears, buried Catholics up to their necks, and played nine pins with their heads." In England, "Bloody Mary" got her name, of course, in the attempt to keep the faith of

England pure for Rome, while in the next century the Puritans under Cromwell sought a church free not only from papal authority but also from other perceived limitations upon Christian practice. Thus, Cromwell's Crusade, taking time to sing Psalm 68—"Let God arise, Let His enemies be scattered"—would not only execute the king but give no quarter to Catholics, slaughtering 3,352 of "the enemy" in a single massacre at Drogheda.[11]

In time, of course, other Puritans would make their way westward across the Atlantic, where other such slaughter of indigenous populations would occur, giving rise within a couple of centuries to the greatest amassing of military might ever witnessed in the pages of human history. Though the Western world would seek to separate religion and politics, and killing for religion would become taboo, Westerners would become more and more convinced that their political traditions were the savior of human history, and democracy and democratic institutions the salvation of the world. And that civilization, convinced with a pious fervor as sure of itself as any Crusader ever was, would become the first, and to this point the only, civilization ever to drop an atomic bomb—twice—on civilian population centers, and that after having burned alive tens of thousands of civilians in firebombing campaigns.

Indeed, may God have mercy, for just as the apostle declared, we are all sold under the bondage of sin, all have fallen short of the glory of God, and the wages of such has indeed been the sowing of death and destruction.

3

Looking for New Testament Christianity

Practicing "double vision," seeking first to understand prior to being understood, is no small endeavor. One of the assumptions that I inherited as an adolescent from the preacher in my home church was this: any number of persons of goodwill can sit together, reason together, and come away agreeing about the meaning of the text of Scripture. If this be true, and if consequently you did not agree with me, then I was left to conclude that you must be under the sway of some wicked prejudice or some malicious unwillingness to do God's will. Thus implied the pulpiteer, or so I concluded. In other words, there was never more than one way to see anything. There was the right way—to which we had access, because we knew that *we* were people of goodwill—and all the other wrong ways. It was a very self-satisfying way to live. Pity all the poor wretches who had not figured out everything I had figured out.

In spite of this, the pews of our church were filled with lots of wonderful folks—caring, kind, and generous, as well as humble, down-to-earth, and simple, in the best sense of the word. There were many virtues lived and thus taught well. Lots of elderly widows who were the embodiment of quiet grace; a postal worker whom I always considered the paragon of kind service; Ms. Daisy, the eldest matriarch of the church, who never had anything but a smile and encouragement, regardless of her own frailties or difficulties. There was something beautiful about growing up in a small conservative church in the American South, before the advent of the fragmentation made possible by our endless technological gadgetry. We took our life together seriously, and we adolescents could call seventy-year-olds "Brother Fields" and "Sister Tumlin." We learned social skills, to say "ma'am" and "sir," and did not think of such practices as hierarchical but just a way to show respect for people who had put in more time in life, had braved more storms, and had thus gained, we trusted, more wisdom than we had yet acquired. We learned to say "hello" to strangers on the street in our small town. This was no pretense but simply a way of treating other people like people rather than some inconvenience on the sidewalk to be ignored. We were taught the art of small talk, an art I would later in life come to appreciate as an exercise in kindness, given that there are very many people who are so very lonely. People in the church made sacrifices for one another. The women, mostly, would cook for the sick and shut-in. Folks would share things out of their gardens with one another and sit in one another's homes on weekend nights and sing hymns. I loved all of that. We thought our community together mattered. And it did.

Restricted Vision

But in the midst of all this goodness, our sights were often restricted. We were unable to see beyond certain ways of reading the Bible or seeing the world. Take "turning the other cheek" and "loving your enemies," for example. When the seventh-grade bully slapped me after I said something about his bullying a classmate, I did not strike back but stayed glued to the bench on which I was sitting. Was it my literal understanding of the teaching of Jesus—"turn to him the other cheek also"—that kept me still, or was it adolescent coward-ice? The bully, as bullies often do, realizing I was not going to hit back, slapped me again. About that time, the PE teacher arrived—a walking mass of muscle—jerked up both of us, as mad at me as he

14

was at the bully, and pulled me off to the side, saying, "Why didn't you hit him back?" Tears in my seventh-grader eyes, I said, "I don't think I'm supposed to."

The teaching of Jesus was simply a rule: do this. But this approach overlooked the possibility that Jesus was teaching not a mere legalistic rule but a skill, a sort of third way between retaliation on the one hand and passivity on the other. It would take listening to other voices before I could construe such texts in a different light. It would be fifteen years later before I learned that "turn to him the other cheek also" was, perhaps, *not* a command to be passive. It may well mean to employ very creative responses to subvert violence.[1] I did occasionally find a creative third way: like the time another bully, sitting across from me, leaned over the cafeteria table and peered into my lunch tray at the dessert he wanted, spat on it, and with a smart-ass grin looked up at me and said, "You want that?" I leaned over my tray, put my mouth close to the dessert into which the bully had just spat, and spat into it myself, and said, "No, I don't want it. Do you?" I smiled back with a smart-ass grin too. It was *not* love of enemy; but it was also not passive acceptance of injustice, even if trivial; and it was also not doing "evil" to him as he did to me.

Years later, I would discover Gandhi's assertion that in the face of social injustice, given the choice between cowardice that yields passivity and bravery that employs violence, he would choose bravery and violence. He further asserted that bravery that gives rise to nonviolent resistance is the best and superior option. But cowardice must first be overcome. It will not do simply to inculcate a legalistic rule, such as "turn the other cheek"; a life of faith requires development of one's moral fiber. In other words, the "right thing to do," considered from a simplistic angle, could mask mere cowardice, *or* it could be an act of great courage.

Beyond these sorts of literalist and legalist readings of the text, though, was another form of restricted view; namely, we failed to see history or society as having much relevance to the story of the New Testament. So while there was much discussion about certain issues of morality—"don't drink, don't dance, don't cuss"—other matters of great social and moral significance received scarcely a single word of attention from the pulpit, so far as I recollect. We lived, for example, in a racially segregated Alabama town, and the racial tension was never far from our consciousness. It was not uncommon to hear white Christians refer to "nigger town." It was rumored among us seventh graders that one of our church members, not a particularly active church member, but a member nonetheless, was a member of the KKK. And one of the bus bombings of the civil rights movement occurred just out on the interstate not more than fifteen or twenty miles from my home. I do not recall having heard the story of that fateful day until after I had gone away to graduate school and had been away from home ten or fifteen years.

Similarly, and in spite of my seventh-grader desire to take "turn the other cheek" seriously, neither do I recollect a single sermon or Sunday school class about war, in spite of the fact that war was undoubtedly on our collective social radar. I was raised at the height of the cold war, when we wondered whether the Russians would obliterate us with nukes one morning while we innocent schoolchildren sat in our classes. We would, on occasion, go sit still in the hallways for drills—we knew either a tornado or a nuclear warhead just might get us one day. (I never understood how sitting in the hallway of a brick building built at the end of the nineteenth century would protect us from a hydrogen bomb. But the drills certainly served the social function of teaching us to distrust, if not hate, the Russians, as well as teaching us how to be fearful. And distrust, hate, and fear are indispensable to power politics, of course.)

We just did not talk in church about such things. There was too much personal morality to be concerned with. And there were all sorts of issues about how to "do church right" that occupied our attention, because the preacher told us that if we did not do those things correctly, we would burn in hell for eternity. And, of course, burning in hell for eternity is worse even than the pain of war and racism, so we paid more attention to what we were told would keep us out of hell. With hell to worry about, there was no time for "social issues" such as war and racism.

Listening to New Stories

Seeking first to understand necessitates that we cultivate the willingness to listen well to other people's stories. So it was that when I encountered stories of individuals from my own heritage who also wanted to take "New Testament Christianity" seriously but who had come to different conclusions about the shape of New Testament Christianity, I started listening. In seminary I began to read tales of our nineteenth-century forebears, who had sought to restore New Testament Christianity as a means of uniting the divided Christian world. And I discovered something quite shocking: that when they sought to restore New Testament Christianity, they often concluded that war-making was alien to such a faith. They were employing a sort of radical conservatism; that is, they insisted that if we take the Bible seriously, we see that the kingdom of God differs from the "kingdoms of this world" in numerous ways, and that love of enemies is one of the indispensable practices of God's kingdom. Moreover, loving enemies, they insisted, means we cannot wage war against them.

This was news to me. Little did I know that my religious forebears had told both Jefferson Davis and Abraham Lincoln that their faith would not allow them to seek to kill either Confederate or Yankee. Little did I know that the US federal government had shut down one of our schools because of its peace witness during World War I. Little did I know about the story of Corbett Bishop, a disciple of Jesus who came from a small church in my tradition not far from my home. Bishop pioneered nonviolent activist techniques later employed in the civil rights movement and was imprisoned for his war resistance. When he went on a hunger strike, the authorities insisted that he eat and drink, but he refused. The authorities put a feeding tube down his nose, and when a cockroach fell into the feeding solution, Bishop's passive resistance continued unabated. Rather than simply reaching up and pinching the tube to stop the roach, he allowed it to continue down the tube into his stomach.[2]

Oh my—I was not only ignorant of these tales but also shocked by them. I would have been tempted to discount them as silly, except, I think, for this: all these stories were couched in the context of seeking to return to the original meaning and practice of Christianity. This bit of "seeking first to understand" then propelled me into looking for earlier tales, of earlier Christian practice.

And again, I was unprepared for what I found.

4

The Early Church and the Jesus Story

Prior to the advent of Christianity there is no record of anyone suffering death for a refusal of military service.

—Roland Bainton *Christian Attitudes toward War and Peace*[1]

The Early Church

Maximilian was twenty-one years old, called up for the draft in the Roman Empire, and brought before Dion, the proconsul of Africa. Maximilian replied, "I am a Christian, and cannot fight. . . . I cannot serve as a soldier; I cannot do evil. I am a Christian." Nonetheless, an officer measured Maximilian's height. He was five feet ten inches tall. Then the proconsul commanded Maximilian to put on the soldier's insignia. Maximilian responded, "I do not want it. I cannot serve as a soldier." The proconsul threatened him with death. But Maximilian continued, "I will not serve. Cut off my head, if that is your will. But I cannot be a soldier for the world, as I am already a soldier for my God."

The proconsul continued to rebuke the young man. The proconsul turned to Maximilian's father, who was a veteran, and told him to instruct his son to accept conscription. The father refused to sway his son's convictions. Then Maximilian replied, "I do not accept the insignia of men; and if you should really mark me, I would tear it up, since it signifies nothing. I am a Christian. I am not permitted to carry a lead ball around my neck [i.e., the leaden insignia with the emperor's effigy], to salute from beneath it the sign of my Lord, Jesus Christ, the Son of the Living God, whom you do not know, but whom God sent for our welfare and who suffered for our sins. All Christians serve Him; we follow Him, the Restorer of life, the Author of our salvation."

The dialogue continued:

Dion: Accept the insignia and serve, lest you die miserably.

Maximilian: I do not die. My name already belongs to my Lord. I cannot serve.

Dion: Consider your youth and serve. For military service is fitting for a youth.

Maximilian: My service is to my Lord. I cannot serve the powers of this world. I have just said that I am a Christian.

Dion: There are Christians who serve as soldiers in the august company of our lords Diocletian and Maximian, of Constantius and Maximus; and they fight.

Maximilian: They know what is best for themselves. I nevertheless am a Christian, and I cannot do evil.

Dion: Those who wage war do evil?

Maximilian: You know what they do.

Dion: Serve, lest your refusal be the occasion for a miserable death.

Maximilian: I shall not die; and if I should depart from this world, my spirit will live with Christ my Lord.

Dion: Strike his name from the roster. Because of your rebellious spirit, you have refused to render military service; and you shall be punished according to your deserts, so as to serve as an example for others. [Reading the decree from the tablet.] Maximilian! Because you have, with a rebellious spirit, refused to bear arms, you shall die by the sword.

Maximilian: Thanks be to God!

Led to the place of execution, he encouraged his fellows: "My dear brethren, endeavor with all your might, that it may be your portion to see the Lord, and that He may bestow upon you such a crown." He then instructed his father: "Give my new clothes, which you have provided for me for the service, to the executioner; and, when I shall receive thee in the company of the blessed martyrs, we may rejoice together with the Lord."[2]

Reflecting upon such accounts, the church historian Roland Bainton makes the shocking claim that "prior to the advent of Christianity there is no record of anyone suffering death for a refusal of military service."[3] And his assertion is all the more important given another little-known "dirty secret" of the Christian tradition, an almost incredible fact that for the first three centuries of Christian history, *there is not a single writing of the early church leaders in which Christians killing in war is permitted; and any time the question is raised, the practice is prohibited.* This majority opinion began to change in the fourth century, when Christianity became legal under Emperor Constantine and then in time became the only legal religion under Emperor Theodosius. But prior to that, for three centuries, all extant writings of the church fathers reject Christian participation in warfare and killing.[4] This does not mean that the practice of the church was uniformly pacifist. "The early church was not unequivocally pacifist in practice, but major theologians did see military life as a threat to Christian ideals," summarizes Lisa Sowle Cahill in her very helpful book *Love Your Enemies: Discipleship, Pacifism, and Just War Theory.*[5]

Bainton's classic work *Christian Attitudes toward War and Peace* provides a helpful survey: in the era up until 170–80 CE, we find no evidence of Christians in the military, and any references by the church fathers are general in prohibiting bloodshed. Following 170–80, Christians are found in the military, but the early church fathers continue to prohibit killing in war, up until the time of Emperor Constantine, in the early fourth century. Bainton summarizes: "All of the outstanding writers of the East and the West repudiated participation in warfare for Christians."[6]

Consider these examples.

In 177 the Christian Athenagoras responded to charges that the Christians were guilty of cannibalism—a wild rumor likely grounded in the Christians' practice of "eating the body and blood" in the Eucharist. His "Plea for the Christians" insisted that Christians could not possibly be guilty of cannibalism, since one must first kill before committing the atrocity of cannibalism. Yet even to witness capital punishment is unacceptable to the Christians: "We cannot endure even to see a man put to death, though justly." The games of gladiators and wild beasts were likewise rejected, for "to see a man put to death is much the same as killing him." The rejection of capital punishment and gladiator games was what we might call a "consistent pro-life ethic," as abortion too was rejected: "We say that those women who use drugs to bring on abortion commit murder, and will have to give an account to God for the abortion." And expectedly, Athenagoras rejects too the practice of infanticide, in which unwanted babies were left to die of exposure to the elements: "Those who expose them are chargeable with child-murder."⁷

Tertullian (ca. 155–240), a convert who had training in the law, claimed that the government of the empire was ordained by God— was ordered by God for God's good purposes. Christians thus could not only honor that function of government, namely to keep order, but also pray for rulers, as Scripture commands. "We offer prayer for the safety of our princes,"⁸ Tertullian claimed. Indeed, "Without ceasing, for all our emperors we offer prayer. We pray for life prolonged; for security to the empire; for protection to the imperial house; for brave armies, a faithful senate, a virtuous people, the world at rest, whatever, as man or Caesar, an emperor would wish."⁹ The despisers of Christians may find such prayers surprising, but Tertullian reminds his readers that Christians are commanded to go "so far as to supplicate God for our enemies, and to beseech blessings on our persecutors."¹⁰ Thus, the persecuting emperor receives the prayers of the church as well.

But in a manner paralleling the New Testament's realism (exhibited in Romans 13 and 1 Timothy 2) regarding the way in which the "powers" and "authorities" serve as a sort of governor restricting the outbreak of chaos and widespread violence, Tertullian also acknowledges the value of the order preserved by the empire. He calls this a "greater necessity for our offering prayer in behalf of the emperors, nay, for the complete stability of the empire, and for Roman interests in general. For we know that a mighty shock impending over the whole earth—in fact, the very end of all things threatening dreadful woes—is only retarded by the continued existence of the

Roman empire. We have no desire, then, to be overtaken by these dire events."[11]

But this acceptance of the role of the empire—in keeping order, analogous to the police function of the modern state—did not mean that Christians could thereby practice warfare on behalf of the empire. Tertullian queried, "If we are enjoined, then, to love our enemies, as I have remarked above, whom have we to hate? If injured we are forbidden to retaliate, lest we become as bad ourselves: who can suffer injury at our hands?"[12] "The Lord, in disarming Peter, unbelted every soldier."[13] Or, he asked, "Shall the son of peace take part in the battle when it does not become him even to sue at law?"[14] For Tertullian, the "principal precept"[15] of the disciple is the command to love our enemies.

Consider these other witnesses. According to Athenagoras, disciples of Jesus "do not rehearse speeches, but exhibit good works; when struck, they do not strike again; when robbed, they do not go to law; they give to those that ask of them, and love their neighbours as themselves."[16] Justin Martyr (ca. 110–65) said, "We who were filled with war, and mutual slaughter, and every wickedness, have each through the whole earth changed our warlike weapons, our swords into ploughshares, and our spears into implements of tillage."[17] And, "We who formerly used to murder one another do not only now refrain from making war upon our enemies, but also, that we may not lie nor deceive our examiners, willingly die confessing Christ."[18]

Clement of Alexandria (ca. 153–217), to unbelievers, proclaimed: "If thou enrol thyself as one of God's people, heaven is thy country, God thy lawgiver. And what are the laws? 'Thou shalt not kill; thou shalt not commit adultery; thou shalt not seduce boys; thou shalt not steal; thou shalt not bear false witness; thou shalt love the Lord thy God.' And the complements of these are those laws of reason and words of sanctity which are inscribed on men's hearts: 'Thou shalt love thy neighbour as thyself; to him who strikes thee on the cheek, present also the other.'"[19] Or Cyprian (200–258) in a treatise on the virtue of patience: "[T]hat you should not swear a curse; that you should not seek again your goods when taken from you; that, when you receive a buffet, you should give your other cheek to the smiter; that you should forgive a brother who sins against you, not only seven times, but seventy times seven times, but, moreover, all his sins altogether; that you should love your enemies; that you should offer prayer for your adversaries and persecutors?"[20] Elsewhere Cyprian observed, "The whole world is wet with mutual blood; and murder, which in the case of an individual is admitted to be a crime, is called a virtue when it is committed wholesale." "And God willed iron to be for the culture of the earth, but not on that account must murders be committed."[21]

Similarly, Dionysius of Alexandria (ca. 200–265) said, "Love is altogether and for ever on the alert, and casts about to do some good even to one who is unwilling to receive it."[22] And Justin quoted Jesus, who "taught thus: 'If ye love them that love you, what new thing do ye? for even fornicators do this. But I say unto you, Pray for your enemies, and love them that hate you, and bless them that curse you, and pray for them that despitefully use you.'"[23]

Arnobius (died ca. 330) interpreted the Pax Romana as the consequence not of Roman might and militarism but of the peaceableness of the Christian communities within the empire's realm:

> For since we, a numerous band of men as we are, have learned from His teaching and His laws that evil ought not to be requited with evil, that it is better to suffer wrong than to inflict it, that we should rather shed our own blood than stain our hands and our conscience with that of another, an ungrateful world is now for a long period enjoying a benefit from Christ, inasmuch as by His means the rage of savage ferocity has been softened, and has begun to withhold hostile hands from the blood of a fellow-creature.[24]

Thus, in spite of the variety of ways in which the early church fathers may make their argument, the varieties of ways in which they accept or critique the empire, we have this consistency *for almost three centuries*: Christians do not kill in war.

Calls for Renewal

There would be many times, in the course of intervening centuries, in which various voices would rise up and call Christians back to nonviolent love of their enemies. The sixteenth-century Radical Reformers, for example: they rejected the co-option of imperial might by both Roman Catholicism and mainstream Protestantism, insisting that the gospel entailed putting away the sword, as Jesus had taught. Michael Sattler was executed for such treason. Sattler and the Anabaptists were hunted like animals by the Christian mainstream. Sattler and his fellows threatened the imperial interests of Western Christianity on a variety of fronts (refusal to take oaths, an insistence upon adult believers' baptism instead of infant baptism, and more), but his nonviolence was particularly repugnant to the authorities, for he insisted that such nonviolence had an impact upon the Christian response to the Turks who threatened from the east. Sattler had taught, said the official charges read against him at his trial, that "if the Turks should invade the country, no resistance ought to be offered them; and if it were right to wage war, he would rather take the field against the Christians than against the Turks; and it is certainly a great matter, to set the greatest enemies of our holy faith against us."[25]

In his response, Sattler said that

> if the Turks should come, we ought not to resist them; for it is written: Thou shalt not kill. We must not defend ourselves against the Turks and others of our persecutors, but are to beseech God with earnest prayer to repel and resist them. But that I said, that if warring were right, I would rather take the field against the so-called Christians, who persecute, apprehend and kill pious Christians, than against the Turks, was for this reason: The Turk is a true Turk, knows nothing of the Christian faith; and is a Turk after the flesh; but you, who would be Christians, and who make your boast of Christ, persecute the pious witnesses of Christ, and are Turks after the spirit.[26]

Sattler's tongue was cut out, his body was torn with red-hot tongs, and he was burned at the stake.

Since such calls for renewal in the sixteenth century, many other voices have been raised in similar fashion: the Quakers; some early twentieth-century Pentecostals; the American civil rights movement that was led by the Baptist preacher Martin Luther King Jr., whose nonviolence was informed by Jesus, a stance which led to King's own death; and numerous others.

But what about the text of the New Testament itself? Does the early historical tradition, and such varied calls for reform, flow from the New Testament? And though the early Christians clearly did not see their nonparticipation in warfare as a merely strategic move but as a principled stance, does this principled position flow from the New Testament itself, or is it merely a historical accident? And more, is the New Testament even *concerned* with such a question, such a *political* question as war?

5

The New Testament
and the Politics of Jesus

The only people on earth who do not see Christ and His teachings
as non-violent are Christians.

—Gandhi[1]

To Istanbul and Back

I thought that the best place to jump into the waters of learning
about Christianity and Islam would be the Middle East. So I went.
I traveled into various hot spots like Hebron and Ramallah. But it
turned out that in these hotbeds of discontent, I was usually more
worried that I would get lost and, typical American traveler that I am,
speaking only English, would find no one who spoke my language,
or that I would encounter one more rug salesman to whom I did not
want to give my afternoon or my money. All the Palestinians I met
were very gracious to the American Christian.

The only time I thought, "Okay, you may very well die right now,"
was just after my arrival in Istanbul. It had been a long day—the
security had been so tight in Tel Aviv that I was irritable with the

long lines and hassles and waiting and questioning and people with guns poking into my luggage. The masked Turkish authorities were taking the swine flu epidemic seriously, with infrared cameras set up just outside passport control, scanning new arrivals for fevers.

But that was not when I thought I might die: it was in the taxi ride from the airport, the Sea of Marmara on my right, the minarets and domes of the magnificent mosques of the historical district appearing in the distance. I caught a glimpse of a speed-limit sign and then realized that our taxi was hurtling down the highway at twice that speed. We slipped through an intersection as the light turned red, and the taxi driver, whose ignorance of English was rivaled only by my ignorance of Turkish, looked at me and shouted with a big grin, "*Olé!*"

Stepping into Istanbul, a magical city, is stepping back in time. It has been the capital city of three great world empires, as the eastern capital of the Roman Empire, the capital of the Byzantine Empire, and the capital of the Ottoman Empire. In Tennessee, something is old if it's been around for a century. In Istanbul, the "New Mosque" is more than four hundred years old. From the terrace of my little hotel downtown, I had a spectacular view of the magnificent Blue Mosque, with its six minarets floodlit at night, and then off to the left the Hagia Sophia, one of the grandest architectural achievements in the Christian tradition, a church building dating back to the early sixth century, built on the site of two even earlier church buildings. (And, the local Muslim Turks are quick to point out, the church's artwork was never destroyed: plastered over, covered over with Islamic inscriptions, but not destroyed, thus honored, and now much of it restored—some of the world's most magnificent mosaics.) Istanbul was long called Constantinople, namesake of the emperor Constantine, who had such a profound impact upon the history of Christianity in the West. Thus, Istanbul is a symbol of the transition in the Christian tradition from persecuted minority to persecuting majority. As the capital city then of the Byzantine Empire, it served as the stage for some of the greatest conflicts between Christianity and Islam. It was the scene of a great showdown between the Muslim Umayyads and the Christian Byzantines, in which the Muslims left defeated. It was a staging ground for the Crusades under the Byzantines. And it would in time become the capital for the Islamic Ottoman Empire, under which it would be renamed Istanbul.

Besides exploring all the architectural gems and museums, I had the privilege of consulting with some faculty at Fatih University, who welcomed me to conversation and lunch. In the early part of our conversation, a Muslim professor, himself a lively advocate of the political superiority of Islam over Christianity, asserted that Christianity was *apolitical* from the start; Islam was not. Since Islam from its very earliest days took politics seriously, it developed rules regarding the conduct of war. Christianity, on the other hand, was not concerned with politics or governance and thus did not establish such rules. Not equipped with the same sorts of limits upon war as Islam, Christians have harshly killed men, women, and children in warfare. Islam has rules about when it is proper to go to war, and when not. Islam has rules about what is and is not acceptable in war. Christianity, because it was apolitical from the start, has none of these rules. Once entangled in imperialist politics, Christians committed all sorts of excesses in war.

Such went his argument. And making allusion to the United States making war upon Iraq, with its supposed justification grounded in Saddam Hussein's having had weapons of mass destruction—all of us knowing at this point that there were no such weapons—someone in the room said, "We know who has weapons of mass destruction, and we know who has been willing to use them."

When I objected, "But there are rules governing the rightful use of war and violence in the Christian tradition," my interlocutor astutely asked, "But where did they get those rules?" That is, he seemed aware that the rules of the Just War tradition did not arise from Christian Scriptures themselves, or from Jesus himself, but from Roman and Greek traditions. So, he continued: Christianity from the start was not political; it became political once involved with the Roman Empire in the fourth century. From that inauguration of Christian imperial politics, one can draw a straight line to the bombing of Hiroshima and Nagasaki, to the mass slaughter of innocents through weapons of mass destruction, and to American imperialistic imposition of its will. So went the conversation.

The Muslim scholars in the room were, on some counts at least, quite correct. But they were wrong in a terribly important point: that early Christianity was "apolitical"; that is, not political. But the irony is deep here—many Western Christians assume the same thing these Muslim scholars assume.

On the Meaning of *Politics*

Of course it all depends upon what one means by *politics* as to whether the early church or the New Testament is concerned with it. In common usage, *politics* simply means conniving, opportunistic manipulation of the mass of people in order to acquire social power, namely, through the mechanism of governmental office. Lacking such cynicism, others assume that *politics* simply comprises positions of power in governmental office. Others have assumed that *politics* is inseparable from coercive power,[2] namely, police or war-making power. In any of these senses, I would agree that Christianity in its earliest strands is indeed not "political."

But if we consider the word *politics* in its classical sense—pertaining to the ordering and arrangement of a human community—then the teachings of Jesus are indisputably political. In other words, any community of people must ask questions regarding the practices and expectations that govern their life together. This is, in the classical sense, politics. If this be our definition of *politics*, Jesus is indisputably "political." How shall we deal with scarcity of goods? Through the practices of trust, working, and sharing. How shall we deal with conflict? Through the practice of it always being "our turn" to initiate a process of seeking reconciliation, whether we are in the wrong or they. How shall we deal with enemies? By praying for them, doing good for them, and giving them drink when they are thirsty. It hardly needs be said but probably must be: this would entail not trying to kill them.

Especially since the time of the Protestant Reformation, the distinction between the "secular" and the "spiritual" has profoundly shaped our reading of Scripture; that is, we have assumed that biblical texts pertain to the realm of the spiritual or personal, while other authorities, such as civil rulers or natural law or some ethic "agreeable to all rational people," will govern the secular realm. But as William Cavanaugh and John Milbank have been teaching us these days, the distinction between the secular and the spiritual as separate spaces was invented. There is no such distinction in the Bible, and this invention has wrought all sorts of mischief in the subsequent interpretation of the biblical texts.

The early church did not trouble itself with asking whether the disciples of Jesus should obey the teachings of the Sermon on the Mount, for example. But in time, this became a hotly debated question. With the rise of Christendom, the sermon's prohibition against self-defense was seen as mandatory for monks or clergy but not required for Christians who held offices that called them to use lethal force for the defense of neighbor. This distinction—some Christians are called to take the sermon seriously and some are not—took a different shape when the distinction between the secular and the spiritual was invented. That dichotomy provided an interpretive lens, in effect, to dismiss or compartmentalize the sermon's teaching. The sermon, with its teaching on love of enemies or doing good to those who do bad to you, was thought to pertain merely to the realm of the spiritual or the personal, not to the realm of the secular or politics.

Hence, the irony of the Muslims who told me Jesus had nothing to say on politics. In our conversation they objected to many of the modern Enlightenment constructs, while they interpreted Christianity through the very Enlightenment constructs they purportedly rejected. But who can blame them? We Christians have been interpreting our own texts in light of these categories for centuries now. Maybe we have been preaching the purported good news of the Enlightenment instead of the Good News of Jesus—maybe because the Enlightenment allows us to compartmentalize Jesus, maybe because a noncompartmentalized Jesus actually scares us to death. Maybe because the Muhammad story, so far as governance and politics are concerned, sounds like better news to us than the Jesus story.

A Thought Experiment: The New Testament as Political Manifesto

Bumper-sticker theology at least has the potential to break through the complacency that assumes Jesus or the New Testament has nothing to say about such things. "Who Would Jesus Bomb?" and "When Jesus said 'Love Your Enemies' I'm Pretty Sure He Meant Don't Kill

Them" are like sledgehammers, doing very poor work at nuanced engagement with serious questions. But they open up this possibility: might indeed the New Testament be a political—as well as a spiritual—manifesto? So I ask you, dear reader, to participate in a thought experiment. Try to assume, for the sake of our experiment, that Jesus is not merely concerned with a compartment we might call the "spiritual" or the "religious." Assume that Jesus intends to be Lord—that is, Supreme Authority—over every realm, aspect, and facet of life. Then, in that state of mind, consider these texts:

> In him all the fullness of God was pleased to dwell, and through him God was pleased to reconcile to himself all things, whether on earth or in heaven, *by making peace through the blood of his cross.*
>
> Colossians 1:19–20, emphasis added

> Let the same mind be in you that was in Christ Jesus,
> who, though he was in the form of God,
> did not regard equality with God
> as something to be exploited,
> but emptied himself,
> taking the form of a slave,
> being born in human likeness.
> And being found in human form,
> he humbled himself
> and became *obedient to the point of death*—
> even death on a cross.
>
> Philippians 2:5–8, emphasis added

> Bless those who persecute you; bless and do not curse them. . . . Do not repay anyone evil for evil, but take thought for what is noble in the sight of all. . . . Beloved, never avenge yourselves, but leave room for the wrath of God. . . . No, "if your enemies are hungry, feed them; if they are thirsty, give them something to drink; for by doing this you will heap burning coals on their heads."
>
> Romans 12:14, 17, 19–20[3]

> [We are] heirs of God and joint heirs with Christ—if, in fact, we suffer with him so that we may also be glorified with him.
>
> Romans 8:17

31

If you endure when you do right and suffer for it, you have God's approval. For to this you have been called, because Christ also suffered for you, leaving you an example, so that you should follow in his steps. "He committed no sin, and no deceit was found in his mouth." When he was abused, he did not return abuse; when he suffered, he did not threaten; but he entrusted himself to the one who judges justly. He himself bore our sins in his body on the cross. . . . Do not repay evil for evil or abuse for abuse; but, on the contrary, repay with a blessing. It is for this that you were called—that you might inherit a blessing.

1 Peter 2:20–24; 3:9

But I say to you, Love your enemies and pray for those who persecute you, so that you may be children of your Father in heaven; for he makes his sun rise on the evil and on the good, and sends rain on the righteous and on the unrighteous. For if you love those who love you, what reward do you have? Do not even the tax collectors do the same? And if you greet only your brothers and sisters, what more are you doing than others? Do not even the Gentiles do the same?

Matthew 5:44–47

There are, of course, serious and substantive questions of interpretation with each of these texts, and a simple list of proof-texts will not suffice, but our agenda here is not to do the serious exegetical work that is required of the church with regard to these texts.[4] Here the observation is simply this: the early church and numerous interpreters and reformers in the two-thousand-year history of Christianity have come back to the sort of conclusion Walter Wink asserts: "Nonviolence is not a matter of legalism but of discipleship. It is the way God has chosen to overthrow evil in the world."[5]

Much work in biblical theology in recent years has made it clear that one of the overarching notions in Scripture is that God is at work in human history through a *people*, a distinctive community that has its own particular, if sometimes peculiar, ways of life together. Moreover, in the New Testament the apostle Paul in particular contends that this community was inaugurated in the scandalous way of the cross. In Jesus and Jesus's cross, God is reconciling all. Given that God, in Christ, is reconciling all, then all those convictions and commitments that alienate and estrange *peoples* from *one another* are also broken down in Christ. Thus, Paul emphasizes that in the cross, God broke down that very powerful socioreligious force of alienation between Jews and Gentiles.[6] This is not merely a *religious* assertion; it is a *sociopolitical* assertion. Those who were counted "God's people" and those who were counted "not God's people" were brought into a "new humanity," a new creation. And not only Jew versus Gentile, but also man versus woman, slave versus free. The way of nonviolent, suffering love has brought about the new community, and is itself a new politics:

> But now in Christ Jesus you who once were far off have been brought near by the blood of Christ. For he is our peace; in his flesh he has made both groups into one and has broken down the dividing wall, that is, the hostility between us . . . that he might create in himself *one new humanity* in place of the two, *thus making peace*, and might reconcile both groups to God in one body *through the cross*, thus putting to death that hostility through it. So he came and proclaimed peace to you who were far off and peace to those who were near.
>
> Ephesians 2:13–18, emphasis added

The Idolatry of the Nation-State

In that same group of Muslim scholars in Istanbul was a Muslim political scientist who claimed that there is no notion of a "state" in Islam: in fact, he said, the very notion of Iran as a Muslim republic is unacceptable in traditional Islam, for the Iranian arrangement has accepted the authority of a state. I am not so sure I understood his point, but he was concerned that traditional Islam not sell out to the notion of a state that descends from the likes of the political philosopher Thomas Hobbes: with Hobbes and other Enlightenment thinkers, the state takes on a given authority that stands above and over other authorities—including religion.

This particular arrangement is seen in the West as a point of superiority over Islam: that Christianity has adapted itself, privatized itself under the authority of the state. But the notion of the *Umma*—the worldwide community of Muslims, which transcends all other ties, including that of local or national governments or citizenship—is actually a construct from which Western Christians have a great deal to learn. Muslims have too often killed Muslims out of their sectarian interpretations of their faith, just as Christians have done the same to Christians. We have assumed that such violent "sectarianism" is a thing of the past for Christians; but what my Muslim host wanted to make clear, and correctly so, I think, is that the violent sectarianism of the nation-state remains alive and well. After the seventeenth century, the state and its purported authority, for example, have led to American Christians and German Christians slaughtering each other, and so on, ad nauseam.

That is, the state takes on an authority that has, historically, divided and alienated peoples one from the other. What many thoughtful Muslims know about the Christian tradition is that the church has too often been co-opted by imperialistic powers—whether Roman or Byzantine or British or American—and thus, rather than *undercutting* the powers that divide and alienate people, has often *served* and been *used by* the powers that divide and alienate. The state becomes that which demands our obedience, teaches its children to pledge it allegiance, wages war over artificial geographical boundaries, requires Iranians and Iraqis and Germans and Americans to kill one another, and requires them to set aside a higher allegiance, whether Muslim or Christian.

Why "Conservatives" Are "Liberals" in Sheep's Clothing

Another way to make this point is to assert something quite counterintuitive: the problem with stereotypical American Christian conservatism is not that it is *conservative*, but that it is *liberal*: that is, it is politically liberal, in affording a status to the state that is not only illegitimate in orthodox Christian theology, but also (at least according to my informed Muslim hosts) in orthodox Islamic theology. By their focus upon the "spiritual," understood to exclude social and historical realms, conservative Christians have often embraced what would have been judged, from the perspective of the early church, to be heresy. My point is not to say that the state or governing authorities have no place within orthodox Christian thought. Romans 13, 1 Timothy 2, and early church fathers such as Tertullian and Origen all have a place for the governing authorities and their employment of force.

Instead, I am suggesting that when we restrict the kingdom of God to a sphere called "spiritual," then other authorities—such as the state, or democracy, or common sense, or universal reason—take the place of the lordship of Jesus when it comes to politics or economics or the wielding of force. (And, it is important to note, the same could be said for stereotypical American Christian liberalism. Speaking in broad strokes, but still strokes that help us see something that is quite problematic: the difference between Christian liberals and Christian conservatives in America is their disagreement on how the US government should run its business. Obsessing over such, American Christians are then unable to question the arrogant conceit of the increasingly imperial state itself, are unable to have any notion that *Jesus* might have something to say to the imperial state's idolatrous trust in its military might.)

If we substitute the interpretive assumption that God works in human history through a people in place of the false assumption of a secular–sacred divide, then the teachings of Jesus and the early church take on an entirely new, fascinating, and potentially troubling shape. The question becomes not whether Jesus's teaching, and the teaching of the early church, was "political." The more difficult question is this: whether or not we will adopt such teaching as *our* political convictions.

There is much more to be said on this point than can be said here. For example, there is the very serious question of the manner in which Jesus's teachings relate to so-called human governments. This question has been answered in a great variety of ways. But suffice it to say here that, speaking in broad generalizations, the early church and many reformers in the Christian tradition since then have insisted that the primary consideration in answering that question is this: whatever one's role, since Jesus is Lord of Lords and Lord over all powers, one must not set aside the teachings and way of Christ in service to that role. For some this has meant nonparticipation in government, and for others it has meant participation but a staunch refusal to systematically set aside Jesus's way in the midst of such service.[7]

Also important to note is this: to say that Jesus's way of nonviolence is the political stance of the church does not mean, then, that the church has nothing to say to governments who do wield such force.

There are plenty of steps that can be made in the right direction, which the church can and should counsel to the powers that are still unable to accept the way of Christ. When there is manifest injustice, killing tens of thousands in response to the deaths of a thousand, or when there is a social policy that is leading to the oppression of communities of peoples, or whatever the case, there is plenty that the church can and should counsel and insist upon.[8]

But the primary point here is this: Jesus's way is indeed *political*. When the early church claimed that *Jesus* is Lord, the Roman culture knew that *Caesar* claimed to be Lord. When the early church claimed *Jesus* to be Son of God, the imperialists touted *Caesar* as son of the gods. When the early church refused to fight the wars of Caesar, the pawns of Caesar realized the political insult that the Jesus-followers posed. And so on into our day, in which the politics of Jesus will challenge numerous facets, commitments, and practices of every human system of government of which I am aware. "Jesus is Lord" is a consummate political statement. To claim Jesus as Lord of Lords and King of Kings is to claim Jesus as the ultimate authority in every realm of life, politics *not* excluded.

Most Muslims have generally known that their faith and politics are inseparable. And that is a story to which we must now turn.

6

The Qur'an and the Politics
of Muhammad

Fight in the way of Allah against those who fight against you, but
begin not hostilities. Lo! Allah loveth not aggressors. And slay them
wherever ye find them, and drive them out of the places whence they
drove you out, for persecution is worse than slaughter.

—Qur'an 2:190–91

So my Muslim Turkish host was wrong in his contention that Christianity was "apolitical." Christianity *was* political from the start. But it was a different *kind* of politics, a sort of politics one finds in no political party these days, a politics of suffering, nonretaliatory love.

But my host also insisted that Islam *was* political from the start and established rules from the time of Muhammad regarding the rightful use of violence and war. So I began my reading of the Qur'an and my queries into biographies of the prophet Muhammad.

Basics of the Muhammad Story

When Muhammad was born in the Arabian city of Mecca around 570 CE, his father had already died. Muhammad's caretaker, his grandfather, also soon died, further complicating Muhammad's plight. But when he was a young man becoming well known as a good steward, a wealthy widow named Khadijah offered him first a job and subsequently her hand in marriage. She was older—apparently he was twenty-five when he married the forty-year-old Khadijah—but in time bore five or six children by him.

By the year 610, the forty-year-old Muhammad was known as a man of honor and high esteem, a reputable merchant who traveled across the Arabian Peninsula and into greater Syria in his pursuit of commerce. He had been for some time retreating outside the Arabian city of Mecca to a cave, where he would meditate. There he began to receive "recitations," which would in time become the text of the Qur'an. Muhammad did not immediately share them with the community at large. But in time, a small number of followers began to accept the revelations as authoritative, and accepted Muhammad's teaching. The insistent monotheism of Muhammad began to be a threat to the paganism of the Arabian tribes; as is most always the case, economics and worship cult were inextricably linked, and thus the vested economic interests were also threatened.

Consequently, the various tribes felt threatened by Muhammad's teaching, and they began to threaten in return. The Quraysh, Muhammad's own tribe and the ruling power of Mecca, began to bring pressure to bear upon Muhammad. His uncle Abū Ṭālib extended protection, as was expected in a clan-based culture, in which protection of one's own, as well as blood vengeance in the case of attack, is part and parcel of the way of life. But those of lower class who accepted Muhammad's message often lacked such protection and were persecuted. So the Quraysh attacked the clans that contained Muslims, "imprisoning them, and beating them, allowing them no food or drink, and exposing them to the burning heat of Mecca, so as to seduce them from their religion. Some gave way under pressure of persecution, and others resisted them, being protected by God."[1]

Throughout all this, Muhammad counseled nonretaliation. He did not permit—the Qur'anic injunction did not permit—the Muslims to strike back or retaliate. But because of the persecution, Muhammad sent some of the Muslims to Abyssinia (in the region of current-day Ethiopia), where the Christian Negus received them hospitably and provided protection, even when the Quraysh sought to have them extradited and brought back to Arabia. This is an important incident, the earliest example of the possibility of peaceable Christian–Muslim coexistence.

In time the Quraysh initiated a sharp economic boycott against the Muslims in Mecca. Abū Ṭālib's protection persevered even in the face of the boycott, but after Abū Ṭālib's death around 619, another uncle rose to the head of the clan and withdrew protection. (This uncle became the only enemy of the Prophet denounced in the Qur'an by name.)[2] Muhammad's attempt to garner protection from a neighboring town led to his being beaten and turned away. Finally, in 621, some from Medina accepted Muhammad's authority as a prophet and pledged their support. The following year, more than seventy Muslims emigrated from Mecca to Medina, and the leaders of Medina formally agreed to Muhammad's own leadership among them, as well as pledged to give him protection.[3] Consequently, Muhammad's followers and finally Muhammad himself made their way to Medina. This significant moment is called the *Hijrah*, the Emigration. The year of the Hijrah (622 CE) became the first year of the Islamic calendar.[4]

An Important Development: Retaliation Permitted

Muhammad's sojourn in Medina signals a very important change in stance toward retaliation: when the Muslims were persecuted in Mecca and had no apparent recourse to protection beyond that of the clan, the Qur'an stipulates that God did not permit retaliation.[5] But in Medina, with a sufficient power base established, this stance changes. The extended passage from one of the early biographers of Muhammad recounts:

> The apostle had not been given permission to fight or allowed to shed blood. . . . He had simply been ordered to call men to God and to endure insult and forgive the ignorant. The Quraysh had persecuted his followers, seducing some from their religion, and exiling others from their country. . . . [In time, God] gave permission to His apostle to fight and to protect himself against those who wronged them and treated them badly. The first verse which was sent down . . . was: "Permission is given to those who fight because they have been wronged. God is

39

well able to help them,—those who have been driven out of their houses without right only because they said God is our Lord. Had not God used some men to keep back others, cloisters [monasteries] and churches and oratories [synagogues] and mosques wherein the name of God is constantly mentioned would have been destroyed. Assuredly God will help those who help Him. God is Almighty. Those who if we make them strong in the land will establish prayer, pay the poor-tax, enjoin kindness, and forbid iniquity" [sura 22:40–42].[6]

In Medina, some of the emigrants began raiding trade caravans from Mecca, which Muslim sources depict as retaliation for the wrongs suffered from the Meccans who had persecuted them and had now broken treaties.[7] In 624 Muhammad led one such raiding party, accompanied by emigrants and other Muslims from Medina. At the Battle of Badr, Muhammad's party fought an army from Mecca that had been deployed to protect a caravan, and Muhammad's party arose victorious, though outnumbered more than two to one (see sura 8). The subsequent Battle of the Trench, which was more significant from a military perspective, led to Muhammad and his followers defeating the Meccans in a battle at Medina.

The original covenant with the inhabitants of Medina allowed Jews to practice their faith unhindered so long as they did not support the enemies of Muhammad and so long as they contributed to the defense of the community. "All believers are bonded to one another to the exclusion of other men. Any Jew who follows us is entitled to our assistance and the same rights as any one of us, without injustice or partisanship." "The Jews have their religion and the Muslims theirs. Both enjoy the security of their own populace and clients except the unjust and the criminal among them. . . . [The Jews have] the same rights and duties as the members of the tribe themselves," and thus they were expected to "bear their public expenses and so will the Muslims." That is, "since the Jews fight on the side of the believers they shall spend their wealth on a par with them."[8] But, as is widely known, the mutually respectful relationship intended in the covenant did not last. Tension arose between the Muslims and Jews, with the Jews accused of conspiring with the Quraysh against Muhammad. Consequently, many Jews were banished from Medina, and in one instance the Jewish males of one tribe were executed and the children and women taken as slaves.[9] (During this time the direction of prayer was changed from Jerusalem to Mecca.)

In time, and through a series of attempts at negotiating differences and difficulties, Muhammad returned to Mecca with a force of ten thousand armed men and took the city without a fight.

Two Different Stories

From this sort of storytelling, one would not be surprised, then, by the sharp contrast between the words of Jesus ("Love your enemies and pray for those who persecute you") or the words of the apostle Paul ("Bless those who persecute you; bless and do not curse them. . . . Beloved, never avenge yourselves"), and the words of Muhammad on retaliation: "O ye who believe! Retaliation is prescribed for you in the matter of the murdered; the freeman for the freeman, and the slave for the slave, and the female for the female. . . . And there is life for you in retaliation, O men of understanding, that yet may ward off (evil)" (2:178–79). Note the assumption in the text that retaliation against wickedness "wards off" evil: indeed, not an uncommon assumption among Western Christians.

It is also worth noting that two important texts in the New Testament also assume the importance of something akin to a legitimate and necessary "police function" of the governing authorities, which parallels in significant ways this contention in the Qur'an. But the apostle Paul assumes in Romans 12 and 13 that the way of the followers of Jesus does not entail retaliation (Rom. 12), while the state may employ police-like force to restrain evildoers (Rom. 13; compare 1 Tim. 2).[10]

Also noteworthy: the Qur'anic demand is not some sort of hard-hearted insistence upon retaliation as such. It appears that the call for retaliation is not taken as an absolute, for the text also concedes, "And for him who is forgiven somewhat by his (injured) brother, prosecution according to usage and payment unto him in kindness. This is an alleviation and a mercy from your Lord. He who transgresseth after this will have a painful doom" (2:178).

Then there is the extended text, very important in the debates, regarding aggressors:

Fight in the way of Allah against those who fight against you, but begin not hostilities. Lo! Allah loveth not aggressors. And slay them wherever ye find them, and drive them out of the places whence they drove you out, for persecution is worse than slaughter. And fight not with them at the Inviolable Place of Worship until they first attack you there, but if they attack you (there) then slay them. Such is the reward of disbelievers. But if they desist, then lo! Allah is Forgiving, Merciful. And fight them until persecution is no more, and religion is for Allah. But if they desist, then let there be no hostility except against wrong-doers. . . . And one who attacketh you, attack him in like manner as he attacked you. Observe your duty to Allah, and know that Allah is with those who ward off (evil). (2:190–94)

Such fighting, both here and elsewhere in the Qur'an, is depicted not as aggressive war but as justified engagement with treaty-breaking persecutors. It seems quite fair to summarize much of the discussion of war in the Qur'an thus: warring and violence are eschewed, but in the face of persecution or oppression, to turn cowardly away from the duty of war-making as a form of redress is to disobey God. Thus, in sura 8, "Spoils of War," revealed in Medina and assuming a backdrop of the Battle of Badr, courage in war is enjoined upon the Muslims: "When ye meet those who disbelieve in battle, turn not your back to them. Whoso on that day turneth his back to them, unless manœuvering for battle or intent to join a company, he truly hath incurred wrath from Allah, and his habitation will be hell, a hapless journey's end" (8:15–16).

Indeed, the fighting of the Muslims is depicted as the fighting of Allah. "Ye (Muslims) slew them not, but Allah slew them. And thou (Muhammad) threwest not when thou didst throw, but Allah threw" (8:17). Thus, the judgment of God and the will of God are discerned in the outcome of the battle. So against the Quraysh, the prominent tribe of Mecca that had opposed Muhammad and purportedly sought a judgment of God against Muhammad, the revelation proclaims, "If ye sought a judgment, now hath the judgment come unto you. And if ye cease (from persecuting the believers) it will be better for you, but if ye return (to the attack) we also shall return" (8:19).

The text goes on to assert that the outcome of a battle—who perishes and who survives—is taken as a "clear proof" of the sovereignty of God (8:42). "O ye who believe! When ye meet an army, hold firm and think of Allah much, that ye may be successful" (8.45). Reflecting the odds overcome by Muhammad in the famed Battle of Badr, the Qur'an proclaims: "O Prophet! Exhort the believers to fight. If there be of you twenty steadfast they shall overcome two hundred, and if there be of you a hundred (steadfast) they shall overcome a thousand of those who disbelieve, because they (the disbelievers) are a folk without intelligence" (8:65).

In this same context arises one of the most important texts in the Qur'an on war: first, it is yet another statement that the desired end is cessation from hostilities. Under certain conditions, war-making is permitted, indeed even required. But when those conditions no longer exist, then warring must cease. Or, if one finds oneself engaged in war because of the justifiable cause of persecution by one's enemies, and then one finds that the persecution ceases, the warring should cease:

> Tell those who disbelieve that if they cease (from persecution of believers) that which is past will be forgiven them; but if they return (thereto) then the example of the men of old hath already gone (before them, for a warning). And fight them until persecution is no more, and religion is all for Allah. But if they cease, then lo! Allah is Seer of what they do (8:38–39).[11]

Similarly: "If they incline to peace, incline thou also to it, and trust in Allah" (8:61). This basic logic of war-making in the Qur'an is the same fundamental logic of the Christian Just War tradition: under certain conditions, war-making is permissible—even required. But when the perpetrators cease in their offense and violence, then the Muslim must also stop the war-making.

The Narrative Logic of the Muhammad Story and the Jesus Story

It is a common myth these days that all religions are specific expressions of the same universal phenomena. If this is assumed, then the next step in such logic is to assert that all religions are basically saying the same thing. But it seems quite clear, with the bit of storytelling and textual examination that I have done here, that the narrative logic of the Qur'an and of the New Testament are *not* "basically the same." The fundamental storyline of the two differs: Jesus comes announcing the kingdom of God, is persecuted for his message, calls his followers also to "take up their cross" and follow in that way, and loves his enemies unto the very point at which they kill him. His early followers, as we have seen, embody this narrative logic in their life together.

Muhammad comes proclaiming the rule of the one God, proclaiming monotheism in the midst of a pagan and warring and unjust culture; is persecuted for his message of justice and mercy; tells his followers not to fight back—for a while—and then, in time, permits the measured use of violent force on behalf of justice. At first accepting the injustice and not fighting back, Muhammad is in time given permission to retaliate. Thus, John Kelsay in his seminal work on war and Islam says that a notion of justifiable war is *"an aspect of the foundational narrative of Islam."*[12]

Jesus, according to some interpreters, grapples with this very same question—in his time of tempting in the wilderness and his time of prayer in the Garden of Gethsemane prior to his arrest and crucifixion—but is not given that permission and goes to his death. Historians may or may not provide background that questions whether my summary storytelling is historically factual; at this point I am interested only in pointing out that if we take the two stories at face value, the basic logic of the two different stories is indeed quite different.

What the Difference Is *Not*

It must be reiterated that to say that these two stories are different does not mean that in Western culture the difference is properly understood. The most common false understanding of the difference is to say that Muhammad was a religious leader *and* a political leader, while Jesus was *only* a religious leader. Those who describe the difference this way are simply saying that (a) Islam is not a Western religion that has accepted the conceits of Western political liberalism, which insists upon the "privatization of religion"; and (b) that Christianity has sold its own soul to Western political liberalism.

Instead, the difference is here: Muhammad and Jesus were *both* religious and political leaders, but Muhammad accepted the employment of armed force and war-making in his administration of justice, while Jesus's kingship necessitated a different sort of politics for the kingdom of God, namely, nonviolent, suffering love.[13]

There *are* clear parallels between Jesus and Muhammad. It is clear from the Qur'an that Muhammad was concerned for a just, orderly, and fair society; and the prohibitions upon usury and interest (which, by the way, were also seen as sinful in the early Christian community) can be seen as an expression that the wealthy not have undue power over the poor. The *zakat*—the required tax or gift or contribution to the poor—is an institutionalized policy representing this concern as well, just as the Jubilee was a parallel institution in the Old Testament, and in the proclamation of Jesus.

Even Muhammad's teaching on women—particularly his regulation of polygamy—was not an objectification of women, but a step or two or three in the direction of the honoring of women. That is, Muhammad's regulations of polygamy (that a man not take another wife unless he can properly provide for her financially, for example) were profoundly "pro-woman" in his Arabian context. It is similar to Moses's *lex talionis*—an eye for an eye, a tooth for a tooth—which when judged by contemporary Western standards seems barbaric; but when judged by a culture that would take much *more* than an eye in retaliation for an eye, and take much *more* than one life in retaliation for one life, then it is seen for what it was: a step in a new, liberating direction. Similarly, I have encountered a number of Muslim writers, both male and female, who note that the extensive covering of women in public is a matter of modesty instead of a matter of oppression. In fact, they turn the Western objections on their head, noting that the lack of modesty in Western cultures leads to a widespread objectification of women, and thus to their oppression—in the name of liberty, no less.

And so we can draw both comparisons and differences between Jesus and Muhammad. There are significant similarities in the proclamation of the lordship of God alone, trumping all other powers and claims for allegiance. A proclamation of the unity of all those who are faithful to this God, a unity that trumps all other allegiances; a concern for the poor and dispossessed; and many others could be enumerated. But note that all these commitments are clearly "political" and "social" practices.

The fundamental *political* difference between the logic of these two stories, I suggest, is at the level of the believers' employment of armed force.

This leads me to a disturbing hypothesis: that the Christian mainstream looks more like the Muhammad story than the Jesus story.

Historical Outcomes as Theological Vindication

Before saying more about this troubling hypothesis, I want to briefly raise an important theological question, which I believe central to the fundamental difference between the Jesus story and the Muhammad story: is it legitimate to interpret the will of God based upon the outcome of a battle, as the Qur'an claims? Obviously, this very move often occurs in the pages of the Old Testament. Indeed, part of the fundamental theological struggle in the pages of the Old Testament is the so-called Deuteronomistic theology articulated in Deuteronomy 26–28, which might be summarized this way: if you do good, you get good, and if you do bad, you get bad, a principle also found in numerous psalms and the book of Proverbs. Of course, the Old Testament itself struggles with understanding this principle as an absolute law, as evidenced in the book of Job. But even more so, if we understand the Christian Scriptures as an unfolding story, revealing to us most fully the will of God in the person and story of Jesus, then we come upon a troubling claim: that God's purposes are revealed in a humiliating defeat of imperial-military crucifixion, not in the victory of a military battle. It is what the apostle Paul will call the "wisdom of God" that is "foolishness" to the world.

As we will explore at greater length later, Islam contends that the prophet Jesus was *not* crucified. Muslims do not reject Jesus's status as a prophet; he *is* accorded prophetic status as a faithful servant of God. But the Qur'an reports that Jesus was not crucified. So far as I know, the Qur'an never specifies any logic or justification for this claim. But if one were to speculate, based upon the larger logic of the Qur'an, then one might think of it this way: the mighty and merciful and faithful God would not and could not have allowed a faithful prophet to have been unjustly killed in such a degrading fashion. It would be foolish that a faithful servant of God should experience such humiliation and defeat.

And to the degree that I have fairly summarized the Qur'anic logic in this regard, to that same degree do we find yet again the deep irony of so many Western Christians who have this very same conviction: that the good guys *ought* to win, because God is on our side. This assumption that the good guys win, must win, should win, is a culturally embedded presumption that extends from the earliest days of the violent Christians who came to the shores of America, to Bob Dylan's satirical "With God on Our Side," to the start of the second Iraq war at the beginning of the twenty-first century.

7

On the Christian,
the Old Testament, and War

I will take vengeance on my adversaries, and will repay those who hate me. I will make my arrows drunk with blood, and my sword shall devour flesh.

—Deuteronomy 32:41b–42

For some years, I was entrusted—or saddled, depending upon how you look at it—with the task of coordinating a twice-per-week assembly for our university student body, in which the purpose of our gathering was to hear and struggle, as a community, with the Bible. During several of those sessions, we grappled with the issue of Christians and war-making. Afterward, an undergraduate student wrote me to protest. The Bible could not possibly call us to nonviolence, he insisted. He enumerated protestations and objections. And if Christianity *does* entail this, he concluded, then just "go ahead and call me a Jew."

Fascinating, on several counts. First, his commitment to the legitimacy of war-making was a more important moral conviction than the lordship of Jesus or the authority of Scripture: if it turns out that Jesus *does* call us to nonviolence, then I'll find some other religion or conviction or authority to support my case, thank you very much. Second, he apparently presumed the Old Testament to be authoritative for contemporary war-making. (Hence, "call me a Jew.")

What of the Old Testament's teaching on war-making?

First, the Old Testament's teaching on war requires us to acknowledge *the necessity of interpretation.* The Bible—given the directions in the Old Testament that seem to contradict statements in the New Testament—requires interpretation. The same can and must be said about the Qur'an. It is not sufficient for us simply to pull texts out of either the Qur'an or the Old Testament and draw our conclusions. There is a history of interpretation and schools of interpretation with which to deal, just as is the case in the Christian tradition. Consider this text:

> As I live forever, when I whet my flashing sword,
>   and my hand takes hold on judgment;
> I will take vengeance on my adversaries,
>   and will repay those who hate me.
> I will make my arrows drunk with blood,
>   and my sword shall devour flesh—
> with the blood of the slain and the captives,
>   from the long-haired enemy.
>
> Deuteronomy 32:40b–42

It is too easy for Christians to assert the alleged peaceableness of Christianity over against the alleged warring tendencies of Islam; simply juxtapose the Qur'an's "slay them wherever ye find them" with the Sermon on the Mount's "turn the other cheek." But one could just as easily juxtapose the Song of Moses from the Book of Deuteronomy, cited above: "I will make my arrows drunk with blood," a text as bloodthirsty, if not more so, than any text in the Qur'an. And note yet another irony: it is not uncommon for Western Christians to (a) cite the Sermon on the Mount; (b) cite the Qur'an's prescriptions for retaliation, and then assert the moral superiority of Christianity as more peaceable than Islam; but (c) when threatened, ignore or compartmentalize the consistent witness of the New Testament regarding nonretaliation and then (d) turn to the Old Testament to legitimate war-making.

But one cannot have one's cake and eat it too.

Second, the Old Testament *model of war is profoundly different from the Just War tradition.* The fact that many Christians, when facing the question of whether war-making is legitimate, run to Old Testament texts simply betrays that Christians have failed to be properly grounded in the Just War tradition (JWT). These two ways of thinking differ on numerous points. As we will see, the JWT sets forward a set of objective criteria that any fair-minded observer should be able to interpret, while the Old Testament model depends upon a leader appointed by God and called by God to war. The JWT requires sharp limits once war has begun, such as immunity of civilians, but the model of war in the Old Testament sometimes rejects such limits and, in some cases, requires the destruction of men, women, and children. (There are cases, as in Deuteronomy 20, in which certain limits are prescribed, such as not destroying fruit-bearing trees; but the same chapter prescribed the killing of men, women, and children that is never permitted in the Christian Just War tradition, a practice that looks like genocide from our contemporary viewpoint. I found no similar injunction for such killing in the Qur'an.) The JWT is thought to be applicable to any nation-state, while war in the Old Testament is in service to the particular mission of Israel.

Third, war in the Old Testament is thus *a function of a geographically located theocratic "state" in the nation of Israel.* Peter Craigie's very helpful book *The Problem of War in the Old Testament* deals with this point at great length,[1] but I shall simply summarize here by noting Craigie's helpful thesis. He maintains that while God is indeed transcendent, God refuses to be removed from the flux and flow of human history. That is, God's *immanence* means that God is involved in the midst of the sin of humans and societies. As such, God cannot be removed from the reality of war. War is always *evil*—and *peace* is the norm and standard in the Old Testament, as evidenced in numerous passages from the prophets—but because of the reality of human sin, and because of Israel's existence as a geographically located state, war is a necessary practice. *But* the story moves beyond this state of affairs, pardon the pun, for in the new covenant, the new manifestation of the kingdom of God is neither geographically nor ethnically located but transcends all such boundaries and borders. If Craigie does not say it outright, he comes awfully close: the project of a *geographically located* manifestation of God's kingdom, a theocratic state, is a failed experiment. Something new arises, and thus the possibility for existence that does not necessitate war. (As an important aside, Craigie notes in his second chapter that the Old Testament has actually had more influence in both Islam and Christianity than in Judaism. After the exile, Israel had no existence as a sovereign state until 1948, at which point secular versions of war-making were again taken up; meanwhile, the Old Testament was co-opted by Christians in pursuit of the Crusades, or in Calvin's Geneva, or in both Confederate and Union forces fighting in the American Civil War.)

Another way of putting Craigie's point is to say that we find in the story of the Bible a developing politics. (Again, it must be reiterated, the development should *not* be described as first political, then apolitical. Instead, the development is from a geographically located and sword-wielding politics to a transnational, ethnically inclusive, towel-wielding politics.) It will not do simply to look for some timeless universal rule, say, extracted from either the Old Testament or the Qur'an, or the New Testament either, without consideration of the context and communal possibilities for practicing such rules.

The early church writers thought not merely in terms of "ethics," of looking for some timeless universal law that all rational people can agree upon. Instead, they thought more in terms of an "alternative politics." That is, their understanding of nonviolence was integrally linked with the mission of the church. In other words, they saw the calling of the church to be a people who embodied, even now, the coming peace of God's reign. Since Jesus the Messiah had inaugurated the kingdom, they could live according to the ways of God's kingdom.

This was, in fact, a terribly important contention. Some critics of the early church charged that Jesus could not have been the Messiah, because the Hebrew prophets themselves had maintained that when the Messiah came, war would be unlearned.

This itself is an observation important for our purposes: when the Old Testament was discussed in light of early Christian faith, the Old Testament was not seen as a repository of texts supporting God-sanctioned crusades against wickedness. When many early church writers appealed to the ancient Scriptures, they understood the overall trajectory to point not toward the ongoing legitimacy of war but toward its rejection. The Scriptures depicted a coming day in which all the arts and industry of war-making would be refashioned into the arts and industry of peacemaking. Thus, the prophet Isaiah, in the eighth century BCE, would declare to Jerusalem:

> In days to come
>> the mountain of the LORD's house
> shall be established as the highest of the mountains,
>> and shall be raised above the hills;
> all the nations shall stream to it.
>
>> Many peoples shall come and say,
> "Come, let us go up to the mountain of the LORD,
>> to the house of the God of Jacob;
> that he may teach us his ways
>> and that we may walk in his paths."
> For out of Zion shall go forth instruction,
>> and the word of the LORD from Jerusalem.
>
> He shall judge between the nations,
>> and shall arbitrate for many peoples;
> they shall beat their swords into plowshares,
>> and their spears into pruning hooks;
> nation shall not lift up sword against nation,
>> neither shall they learn war any more.
>
> Isaiah 2:2–4; cf. Micah 4:1–4

Or again, Isaiah anticipated the day of restoration of Israel in which one (or ones, or a new people) would come, and "the spirit of the LORD shall rest on him, the spirit of wisdom and understanding," one whose "delight shall be in the fear of the LORD." Righteous judgment for the poor, equity for the meek, and judgment upon the wicked would give rise to the reversal of the apparently inherent order of violence in the creation (Isa. 11:1–5):

The wolf shall live with the lamb,
　　the leopard shall lie down with the kid,
the calf and the lion and the fatling together,
　　and a little child shall lead them.
The cow and the bear shall graze,
　　their young shall lie down together;
　　and the lion shall eat straw like the ox.
The nursing child shall play over the hole of the asp,
　　and the weaned child shall put its hand on the adder's den.
They will not hurt or destroy
　　on all my holy mountain;
for the earth will be full of the knowledge of the LORD
　　as the waters cover the sea.

Isaiah 11:6–9[2]

Pagan and Jewish critics of the early church employed such texts against the early church. The prophets themselves, it was objected, maintain that the appearance of the Messiah would usher in the age of peace, that war-making would be unlearned. Clearly, continued the critics, the nations continue to wage war. Jesus could not therefore possibly have been the Messiah. Remarkably, a significant number of early Christians address this question. And their answers come together here: yes, Jesus was the Messiah. And the community of disciples has unlearned the ways of war and learned the ways of peace: the very peaceableness of the church is concrete evidence that Jesus is the Messiah.[3]

One devastating and potential implication of this early church apologetic might be this: *for contemporary Christians to argue that the Old Testament legitimates war-making is to argue that Jesus was not the Messiah. The interpretive move to make the Old Testament the authority for war-making, from this early-church perspective, is to reject the lordship of Jesus.*

Another way to look at this irony can be seen in the charge made by Celsus, that rabid pagan critic of early Christians and lover of the empire. Celsus angrily denounced the church: "If all were to do the same as you, there would be nothing to prevent [the emperor] being left in utter solitude and desertion, and the affairs of the earth would fall into the hands of the wildest and most lawless barbarians; and then there would no longer remain among men any of the glory of your religion or of the true wisdom."[4] Here one finds on the lips of an ancient pagan the very logic employed by American Christians to legitimate participation in American war-making. Imperial existence is thought to be the necessary condition for the existence of one's "religion," unaware of the fact that the "religion" of Jesus is actually the new politics that will ultimately triumph over all imperialisms.

8

The Early Muslims
and the Muhammad Story

My reading of the Qur'an and the story of Muhammad described
in a previous chapter leads then to this conclusion: war is seen not
as a tool of imperial domination but as a mechanism that must be
employed when justice demands it. The Qur'an exhibits no penchant
for bloodthirst but *is* straightforward about employing retaliation and
war in response to aggression, persecution, and treaty-breaking—but
for the sake of peace, not for the sake of retribution.

But what of the unfolding Islamic tradition? Is the unfolding tradition and the classical understanding of war—with its domination and expansion northward—not a better gauge of what is truly
"Islamic"? What is the shape of this "justifiable war"? What are its
goals and means and limits?[1]

The Classical Position on War in Islam

It is well known that Islam spread rapidly in the generations following
the death of Muhammad. How might we understand this spread,
and what should we learn from the fact that it was facilitated by war?

In the early generations following Muhammad's death, Islam moved rapidly into the power vacuum created by the wars between the nominally Christian Byzantine Empire and the Persian Sassanid Empire. The Arabs, united by their Muslim faith, now no longer focused upon fighting one another, expanded with a new singleness of purpose northward, into the power vacuum. But the Muslims did not, as we will see, indiscriminately slaughter nonviolent Christians as they made their way northward. It was instead an encounter of empires, especially the Byzantine Christians and the Muslim Abbasids. And as is always the case, it is difficult to disentangle various imperial elements from the practice of the faith, both in Muslim and in Christian tradition. After reading one of the biographies of Muhammad, Gandhi would assert, for example, that

> I became more than ever convinced that it was not the sword that won a place for Islam in those days in the scheme of life. It was the rigid simplicity, the utter self-effacement of the Prophet, the scrupulous regard for his pledges, his intense devotion to his friends and followers, his intrepidity, his fearlessness, his absolute trust in God and his own mission. These and not the sword carried everything before them and surmounted every obstacle.[2]

Whatever the case, when the Muslims swept northward, the Byzantine Christians they encountered had long ago forgotten the early church's prohibition of war-making and were quite ready to take up the sword against the Muslims. Some Christian communities were so disgusted with the imperial politics of the Byzantines that they welcomed the new Muslim rulers. "The Byzantine state had ruled its eastern subjects in these areas with an authority that was often experienced as ruthless and oppressive. Thus it was that many Oriental Christians welcomed Muslim political authority as a relief from Byzantine oversight and taxation and cooperated with their new Muslim rulers, one of the most important factors in the remarkable ease with which Islam was able to spread across Christian lands. The dhimmi status was preferable to Byzantine oppression."[3]

In this new context, it became common to think of two ways for humankind to exist: that of heedlessness or ignorance (*al-jahiliyya*) or that of submission (*al-islam*). John Kelsay helpfully compares the state of *al-jahiliyya* to Thomas Hobbes's description of the state of nature as "solitary, poor, nasty, brutish, and short." Of course, Hobbes would go on to posit that human community thus necessitated a legitimate authority to wield violence, namely, the state. Otherwise, there would simply be a war of all against all. Classical Islamic tradition believes that *al-jahiliyya* represents a similar condition. However, the solution is not the state, but rather *al-islam*, that is, submission to the good will of God. For Hobbes, the state restrains wickedness and chaos and makes society possible, while for classical Islamic tradition, submission to the will of God makes a just social order possible.

This then gives rise to the classical distinction between *dār al-Islām* and *dār al-Harb*: the territory of Islam roughly correlates with a region in which the head of governance is somehow affiliated with or supportive of Islamic convictions and values. This does not rule out what we may call "religious pluralism." This is evidenced in the very earliest treaty at Medina, as previously noted, and is witnessed in various manifestations throughout Islamic history. "The Sunni view of peace explicitly provides for religious pluralism through the notion of 'protected' religious groups (called *dhimmiyya*) who enjoy relative freedom so long as they pay tribute and thus acknowledge Islamic sovereignty."[4] The territory of Islam thus serves as a theoretical construct to represent a human society that seeks justice and order. But the territory of war, heedless and ignorant, revolves around disorder and strife and injustice. It always exists as a threat to the order and peace of the house of Islam. Consequently,

> the peace of the world cannot be *fully* secure unless all people come under the protection of an Islamic state. Thus there always exists an imperative for Muslims: to struggle to extend the boundaries of the territory of Islam. This is the Muslim way—the "natural" way—to fulfill the trust given to humanity by its creator: to establish peace with justice within a secure political order.[5]

Thus arises the call to jihad: to struggle for the conquest of ignorance and heedlessness. How does this occur? As numerous commentators note, it is clear that *jihad* does *not* mean "holy war" or even "war" or "battle." Instead, it is more accurately translated as "effort" or "struggle." Muhammad is claimed to have taught that "it is the duty of every Muslim to command the good and forbid the evil with the heart, the tongue, and the hand (or sword)."[6] The "greater struggle" is with the human heart itself.[7] Struggle with the tongue entails missionary efforts at preaching. And struggle with the hand includes the use of armed force. Thus, the jihad is to struggle to bring about the good that accords with God's will.

In other words, "peace" is thought to be inseparable from a community that practices justice. Peace is not merely the avoidance of conflict but the proactive establishment of a community that is characterized by justice and assumes that the use of military might is a legitimate component of such a pursuit. The "best guarantee" of such a peace is, of course, a society in which there exists *al-islam*, that is, a submission to the will of God. Thus, the spread of Islamic society is for the good of justice and peace. While in Western political traditions the "will of God" is typically reserved to the realm of private spirituality and is thought to be either above reason or opposed to reason, in classical Islamic thought, the "will of God" is consistent with the universal good of humankind. That is, one cannot speak of what is good for humanity without speaking of the will of God.

With our Western conceits, it would be easy to conclude that this conception is simply "religious war" in the sense of making "converts" through war. On the one hand, jihad as war is inseparable from the Muslim's understanding of God's will. But on the other hand, jihad as war is not the same thing as attempting to "convert" the enemy through war. "There is no compulsion in religion," says the Qur'an (2:256), and the classical Islamic tradition understood quite well that unwilling faith is no acceptable faith at all. (And, as already indicated, the original covenant at Medina clearly stipulated that Islamic rule did not necessitate forced conversion but protected the religious practices of the Jews.) Nonetheless, war could be employed as a "possible and useful means of extending the territory of Islam and thus a tool in the quest for peace."[8] Consequently, war could be rightly waged when there was a just cause (often understood as the need to extend the territory of Islamic rule), a declaration of Muslim intentions to wage war unless the enemy submit, "right authority" in the sense of a legitimate ruling authority, and when the war is fought in a manner befitting the values of the Muslim community (such as *not* fighting for personal benefit or glory but for the good will of God, to bring about peace). And as Kelsay summarizes, "The formal parallels between these rules of war and the Western just war criteria are rather striking." He rightly notes that sometimes the particular *content* of those rules may differ, but nonetheless, the formal logic exhibits striking and noteworthy parallels.

A crucial text for the classical Muslim scholar's reflection upon this question of the legitimate means employed in war is the following account:

> Whenever God's Messenger sent forth an army of a detachment, he charged its commander personally to fear God, the Most High, and he enjoined the Muslims who were with him to do good.
> He said:
> Fight in the name of God and in the path of God. Fight the *mukaffirun* [unbelievers, ingrates]. Do not cheat or commit treachery, and do not mutilate anyone or kill children. Whenever you meet the *mushrikun* [idolaters], invite them to accept Islam. If they do, accept it and let them alone. You should then invite them to move from their territory to the territory of the émigrés. If they do so, accept it and leave them alone. Otherwise, they should be informed that they will be in the same condition as the Muslim nomads in that they are subject to God's orders as Muslims, but will receive no share of the spoil of war. If they refuse, then call upon them to pay tribute. If they do, accept it and leave them alone.[9]

In his seminal work *Arguing the Just War in Islam*, Kelsay notes that this very important text was foundational for the developing Islamic tradition on war-making. Like all traditions, the Islamic tradition surrounding the legitimate methods, means, and conditions for war-making is complex and multifaceted. But Kelsay documents at length that the Muslim scholars developed a variety of criteria and limits upon war, as the above text indicates, and that their criteria paralleled in many ways the Christian Just War tradition. There must be a legitimate authority; there must be just cause; there must be a righteous intention; noncombatants, especially women, children, the elderly, and slaves, are not to be targeted in war. At the same time, Kelsay documents that changing sociopolitical circumstances result

59

in developments and reassessment of the precedents that had gone before, so that the "Islamic conception of war" is dynamic and fluid, changing with its context.[10]

But Is It Really?

Of course, Kelsay's thesis—that there are substantive parallels between the classical conception of war in Islam and the Christian Just War tradition—is a provocative one that not all interpreters buy. Even the American Muslim Louay M. Safi, who holds a PhD in political science and is a former president of the Association of Muslim Social Scientists, as well as former director of research at the International Institute of Islamic Thought, is more critical of the "classical conception" than Kelsay and argues a *discontinuity* between the teachings of the Qur'an and the classical conception. Safi's interpretation is no doubt disputed as well, but he sharply criticizes the "classical doctrine," which he says "mistakenly perceives war as the instrument of the Islamic state to expand the Muslim territories and dominate non-Muslim states." Instead, says Safi, the Qur'an teaches that the proper "aim of war is to assure justice and abolish oppression and tyranny."[11] That is, Kelsay (and convincingly so, I think) argues that the classical conception of war in Islam does parallel the Christian Just War tradition; but Safi insists that one must go back further in Islamic history, to Muhammad and the Qur'an, to understand the parallels between the two, given that the classical era of Islamic conquest is so indebted to imperialist pursuits.

So Safi insists—as I have found numerous Muslims to also insist—that jihad in the Qur'an is never "holy war" in the sense of "a war to enforce one's religious beliefs on others. Most Muslims would reject the equation of jihad with holy war, and would insist that a better description that captures the essence of the Islamic concept of jihad is a just war,"[12] while a "tiny minority of intellectuals" still interpret the Qur'anic prescriptions for jihad as a "divine license to use violence to impose their will on anyone whom they could brand as an infidel, including [some] fellow Muslims." But, he insists, this is not and should not be understood as the normative doctrine of war in the earliest Muslim teaching.[13]

Safi does say what numerous scholars say, regardless of their conclusions: the problem is exegetical. That is, in any community that takes a text seriously, there necessarily arise difficulties of interpretation. All texts are related, in some fashion, to historical context. Therefore the question arises of how the (different) original historical context influences the application of the authority of that text in one's own (different) contemporary context. This problem arises as much in the "secular" interpretation of the Constitution in the United States Supreme Court as it does in any "religious" community, Christian or Islamic or Jewish. As a consequence, the understanding of war—both in Christian and in Islamic communities—is never monolithic, but varying and diverse, dependent upon many variables, but especially the hermeneutical presuppositions one carries to the authoritative text. So Safi on thinking about war in Islam: the "misunderstanding . . . is essentially a problem of textual explication. It is a problem of how a Qur'anic text is and ought to be interpreted."[14] Kelsay documents the same truth with regard to the precedents established in the classical era.

What to Make of the Parallels?

For our purposes, I think three important observations are in order.

First, an observation about what causes are seen as justifying war. As we saw above, the Islamic conception of the state of *al-jahiliyya*—the heedlessness and ignorance in the *dar al-Harb*, in the territory of war—is a threat to the security of the *dar al-Islam*, and thus a justifiable cause for war. This is understandable at one level: all societies have *some* conception of what a "just social order" entails, and all geographically located societies of which I am aware have employed armed force in service to the defense and security of that "just social order," for better or worse. Islam has conceptions, too, of what a just social order entails; and if a just social order, defined by those conceptions, is brought to a region characterized by ignorance and heedlessness and idolatry, then this would be seen as a natural good for humankind. First seek to do so by persuasion, but war is a legitimate last resort.

This position is coherent, of course, but I still find it to be a troubling element of the Islamic tradition, precisely because it seems to leave the door open to all sorts of justification for war-making. A justified war need not be strictly defensive, and Islamic "expansionism" remains a theoretical possibility. But then again, this is precisely the problem that so many Muslims see with Western colonialism and American imperialism: various regimes and countries and regions have been seen as a threat to European or American interests, or more, have been seen as a desired resource for Western interests, and thus war has often been employed in service to the expansion of Western interests. Our American conception of a just social order entails free-market economies and democracy; many believe this to be the natural good of humankind, and clearly our military might has been employed in service to these institutions. So while I look askance at the classical Islamic conception of war—and look with some suspicion at the notion that appears to pervade many contemporary Muslim thinkers, namely, that an Islamic social order is the source of defining a just social order—I cannot but also look suspiciously upon the claims of someone like Woodrow Wilson, who claimed that World War I was the war to end all wars. Wilson and Muhammad both believed that their own social systems were for the good of the world, were (for lack of a better term) historical saviors, and were thus legitimate ends for which the means of war could be employed.

A second observation pertains to noncombatants and the protection of civilians. Kelsay clearly documents the ongoing questions about proper restraint and criteria for the engagement of war in the Islamic tradition. But he also documents another phenomenon that parallels Western developments, namely, the manner in which "military realism"—that is, the demand for effective military strategies—impinges upon the criteria. As we will see in the next chapter, the Christian Just War tradition has maintained that the military must not target civilians. In parallel fashion, the classical Islamic rules of war prohibited targeting women, children, the elderly, the insane, and slaves. Such rules stand in continuity with the Qur'an, which stipulates that there are indeed certain boundaries beyond which it is not legitimate to pass: "Fight in the path of God those who are fighting you; but do not exceed the bounds. God does not approve the transgressors" (2:190).[15]

But, as one classical text queried, can Muslims attack a city when women, old men, slaves, or children are in the city? Or what if the city is holding Muslim prisoners of war? Yes, such attacks are permitted, stated al-Shaybani, a leading scholar of his day, for "if the Muslims stopped attacking the inhabitants of the territory of war for any of the reasons that you have stated, they would be unable to go to war at all, for there is no city in the territory of war in which there is no one at all of these you have mentioned."[16] This, of course, parallels the notion in Western thought that so long as one does not *directly* target noncombatants, then the attack may be justified. "Collateral damage" becomes the term applied to women, children, and old men killed by our bombs and is deemed justified because a military target was in their midst.

This slippery contention also relates to contemporary Muslim militants. As we will see in the discussion below regarding Osama bin Laden, the line between combatants and noncombatants grows blurry. The American Civil War blurs the line when William Tecumseh Sherman depicts the war not merely as a war between two armies but between two societies and sets out upon his forays of destruction across the American South; similar logic is used in the total devastation visited upon German and Japanese cities by the Allies in World War II; and Osama bin Laden will make the same move to justify his slaughter of civilians in the US.

A third observation flows from the second: Kelsay demonstrates that the contemporary Muslim militants, though they have blurred the line with regard to combatants and noncombatants, are nonetheless still engaged in an argument over justifiable war. Muslim militant documents are, at a fundamental level, an argument over "just authority," that is, the question of who may legitimately declare war. Given that the Muslim militants believe that established power structures are corrupt and unfaithful to Islamic teaching, they are convinced of the necessity and justification of revolt against those authorities in order to establish a just social order.[17]

To summarize: we find in the unfolding Islamic tradition a basic logic that runs this way: justice sometimes requires armed force and war; under certain conditions, and within certain restraints, for the purpose of establishing justice and peace, war is permitted, if not required.

And once the Christian tradition gets access to some of the reins of imperial power, its logic on war begins to parallel this Islamic conception of war, the story to which we now turn.

9

The Constantine Story
and the Christian Just War Tradition

That was an apt and true reply which was given to Alexander the Great by a pirate who had been seized. For when that king had asked the man what he meant by keeping hostile possession of the sea, he answered with bold pride, "What thou meanest by seizing the whole earth; but because I do it with a petty ship, I am called a robber, whilst thou who dost it with a great fleet art styled emperor."

—Augustine, *The City of God*

As we have seen, many of the early Muslims believed war to be a means of administering justice and making space for the administration of a community ordered according to the will of God. This conviction began with Muhammad and was carried on into the early generations of Muslims. Thus, their war-making and vengeance-taking are understood to be justified and as a part of the natural ebb and flow of one social order taking the place of others less just and more heedless. Without such armed force justly employed, mosques, churches, and synagogues are destroyed, and humankind hurtles headlong toward destruction.

We have also noted that for the early generations of Christians, a different ethic was employed altogether: appealing to the authority of Jesus, the early church generally believed its vocation did not entail waging the wars of empires, no matter how just. They had a different vocation, a different politics, namely, to embody the peaceable reign of God that had been inaugurated in Jesus of Nazareth, who himself incarnated the peaceable will of God, loving even unto death, and triumphing over the powers in his shameful crucifixion. The "wisdom of God" was foolishness to the world but was nonetheless the power unto the saving of the world. It was patient, suffering love, not justifiable war that would save the world.

Still, according to both the New Testament and the early church fathers, who rejected war-making as legitimate for Christians, the "principalities and powers" had their place in the sovereignty of God. The "powers" were "ordained by God" and would wield the sword—which might be better translated into today's equivalent as the policeman's baton or sidearm, instead of the cruise missile or long-range bomber—on behalf of keeping order. Romans 13 and 1 Timothy 2 assume that the kings and rulers are to check chaos and do provide a function in the basic ordering of society. The "powers," to use John Howard Yoder's metaphor, are like the ushers at a stage show; they serve the important function of helping maintain order, but they are not the show themselves. It is the disciples of Jesus, embodying the peaceable, suffering love of God, who are onstage, the musicians in the performance of God's work in the world. The fact that the powers may assist in "ushering" is insufficient justification for disciples of Jesus to go running after this role if it required setting aside the way of Christ; disciples have a different vocation.[1]

And one may further contend that the legitimate "police function" of the governing powers does not lead inexorably to the legitimacy of war-making. Policing keeps order and checks chaos. War, on the other hand, creates chaos and employs disorder and destruction. Policing seeks to single out the perpetrator of a crime, while war targets people not directly responsible for a crime. Policing, when on the relatively small number of occasions it does use lethal force, is under rules of review and stringent due process, while killing in war lacks such oversight. And so on.

The Rise of Christian War-Making

Things changed and, within a brief period of time, a new concensus arose among Christians in their thinking about war.

There in Istanbul, as well as in the Old City of Jerusalem, one can still see historical artifacts that date to the change in social status for the Christian church: in the "holy sites" identified in Jerusalem by Constantine's mother, or at the Column of Constantine erected in 330 CE to inaugurate Constantinople, the city we now call Istanbul, as the new capital of the Byzantine Empire. For good or for ill, rightly or wrongly, Constantine is considered a figure who had a most profound impact upon the history of Christianity in the West; the Christian community, once an illegal minority and sometimes persecuted, became not only legal but affiliated with imperial power politics.

So, yet another finding surprised me. The shift from Mecca to Medina signals a shift from nonretaliation to justified war-making, just as the shift from early church to post-Constantinian church signals a parallel shift in the Christian tradition. The "Constantinian turn" is analogous to Muhammad's turn; as the Muslim community gets access to power in Medina, Muhammad advocates justified retaliation. As the Christian community gets access to imperial power in and through Constantine, a new consensus arises: Christians may, under certain conditions, legitimately participate in war.

The Logic and Criteria of the Just War Tradition

Formally, the shape of the new logic would parallel what Muhammad had taught.[2] In fact, it would parallel what the best of Greek and Roman logic had also maintained—we might say, what all the "greatest" empires have maintained, that power cannot be used in gross excess but must be used with moderation and restraint, according to one's understanding of what makes for justice. Thus, the famous Roman lawyer and orator Cicero maintained that there was a "natural law" that all humankind, through the use of innate reason, could discern and thus know right from wrong. This natural law applied to nations and their employment of the sword. He thus provided a framework for thinking about "just war," which entailed certain duties and commitments.

There are certain duties that we owe even to those who have wronged us. For there is a limit to retribution and to punishment; or rather, I am inclined to think, it is sufficient that the aggressor should be brought to repent of his wrongdoing, in order that he may not repeat the offence and that others may be deterred from doing wrong.

Then, too, in the case of a state in its external relations, the rights of war must be strictly observed. For since there are two ways of settling a dispute: first, by discussion; second, by physical force; and since the former is characteristic of man, the latter of the brute, we must resort to force only in case we may not avail ourselves of discussion. The only excuse, therefore, for going to war is that we may live in peace unharmed; and when the victory is won, we should spare those who have not been bloodthirsty and barbarous in their warfare.[3]

Here already are some of the criteria of the Christian Just War tradition: war should not be entered hastily but as a last resort when nonviolent methods have failed; the goal is not war-making itself but an establishment of a relative peace; and appropriate treatment must be given to those defeated in war. Cicero goes on to insist that those enemy combatants who surrender must be protected and that war cannot ever be justified unless there is first a declaration of war following the enemy's refusal to satisfy stated objectives.

When Augustine of Hippo articulates criteria for Christians to participate in a justifiable war, he adopts the earlier philosophical position of the Greeks and Romans. Augustine does *not* adopt these criteria from either the New Testament *or* the Old Testament. His criteria are not *biblical*; they are philosophical and theological teachings from other traditions, adapted for the new social standing of the church.

While Augustine articulates a carefully reasoned justification for Christians participating in what he believes to be the sad and sinful necessity of warring, it is most important to note that he is no imperial flag-waver and no zealous patriot. It is a long way from Augustine's lamentation of the occasional necessity of taking up the sword to Nashville country music's belligerent militarism following 9/11, in which Toby Keith equates the way of America with kicking someone's ass.[4] The degree to which Augustine's stance differs from the machismo of American culture may also be located in the fact that *Augustine rejects self-defense* as having any legitimacy in Christian discipleship. Lisa Sowle Cahill summarizes:

His general position on war can be summed up thus: Augustine was willing to commend the use of violence if undertaken at the behest of a legitimate civil authority (understood to have authority from God), if necessary to punish crime or to uphold the peace, and if the combatants intended to establish justice rather than hatefully to inflict suffering on their enemies. Augustine relegated most practical implications of Jesus' "hard sayings" (Matt. 5:38–48) to the Christian's personal affairs, there excluding killing in self-defense. To kill to save one's own life represents an inordinate attachment to a personal temporal good rather than to God's will; but to kill selflessly for the common good may be justified because the good of all is greater than that of one.[5]

When critics claimed that Christianity's "slave mentality" and longing for another world made the empire susceptible to the barbarian invasions, Augustine turned the critique on its head: Christianity is not to blame for the demise of Rome, but Rome's own grasping imperialism. By grabbing for more and more, provocation results and wars are incited. "What are kingdoms," asks Augustine, "but great robberies?"

> Justice being taken away, then, what are kingdoms but great robberies? For what are robberies themselves, but little kingdoms? The band itself is made up of men; it is ruled by the authority of a prince, it is knit together by the pact of the confederacy; the booty is divided by the law agreed on. If, by the admittance of abandoned men, this evil increases to such a degree that it holds places, fixes abodes, takes possession of cities, and subdues peoples, it assumes the more plainly the name of a kingdom, because the reality is now manifestly conferred on it, not by the removal of covetousness, but by the addition of impunity. Indeed, that was an apt and true reply which was given to Alexander the Great by a pirate who had been seized. For when that king had asked the man what he meant by keeping hostile possession of the sea, he answered with bold pride, "What thou meanest by seizing the whole earth; but because I do it with a petty ship, I am called a robber, whilst thou who dost it with a great fleet art styled emperor."[6]

There is, nonetheless, Augustine argues, justifiable war. Being at peace is much preferred, and war is wicked. But the relative merits of a case, in the end, provide the root justification for war as a regrettable necessity. "It is the wrongdoing of the opposing party which compels the wise man to wage just wars." But this is never to be celebrated: to wage justifiable war is a necessity of the sinful nature of human existence and is thus always to be lamented. "Let every one, then, who thinks with pain on all these great evils, so horrible, so ruthless, acknowledge that this is misery. And if any one either endures or thinks of them without mental pain, this is a more miserable plight still, for he thinks himself happy because he has lost human feeling." [7] The celebratory ticker-tape parade, one thinks, would be nigh unto sinful for Augustine: even when "just," war is a matter of great misery, a necessity of the sinfulness of humankind.

Here is a virtue to celebrate: while it seems that Augustine has moved far beyond the teaching of the New Testament and the practice of the early church; while he, like many Christians since his day, became convinced that love of neighbor entails the judicious use of the sword and martial might; he has not, however, fallen prey to the flag-waving and "love it or leave it" nationalism that has too often captured the American church. Would that those churches and disciples who claim to adhere to the Just War tradition also adhere to Augustine's political realism that critiques the vain, arrogant, and prideful exertion of will and grasping after wealth that characterizes imperialistic politics.

Out of the early teaching of Augustine and his bishop, Ambrose, a tradition arose around Christian understanding of warfare. The ethicists thus call it the Just War Tradition (JWT), not as to say with careless manner, "it's just war, it's merely war," but to say that on occasion war is thought justifiable. As in any tradition, there are differences of opinion and arguments, but there is nonetheless a discernible direction of thought and practice. That discernible direction of thought and practice starts with the assumption that war is a regrettable necessity. Certain criteria specify *when* it is legitimate to go *to* war (called the *jus ad bellum*) and *what* it is legitimate to do *in* war (called the *jus in bello*). In addition, there are a number of procedures and considerations of *due process* that should govern the entire endeavor. Given that the JWT is a living tradition, the various rules and considerations have grown and expanded and have been adapted to meet new circumstances. But here is one representative list:[8]

Jus ad Bellum

- Legitimate authority. War must be declared by a rightful authority, such as a duly elected president, a legitimate monarch, or an act of a legislature.
- Just cause. War must be engaged for some substantive reason, such as self-defense, or defense of a third party, or the restoration of order.
- Right intention (objectively understood). War must be undertaken for the intention of restoring peace, of making the world, as a whole, better off than it was prior to the engagement. Thus, it would be illegitimate to engage hostilities because of strategic concerns for resources or military advantage.
- Right intention (subjectively understood). War must be undertaken out of love for the oppressed, and even with an attitude of love for the enemy. While there may be a just cause, to wage war out of vengeance, hate, and resentment means that one fights sinfully. This sometimes is understood to require mercy following the war.

Due Process

- Last resort. All reasonable possible means for reconciliation and restoration should be attempted prior to the start of hostilities. If war is engaged, then the goals of the war must be published for the sake of accountability.
- Sue for peace. The enemy must always be allowed to "sue for peace" on the basis of the stated goals of the war. That is, the enemy must be allowed to enter negotiations to bring about the end of hostilities. Thus, a demand for "unconditional surrender" is unacceptable.
- Winnable. If a war is not, according to one's best understanding, winnable, then it should not be engaged. This points again to the honorable moral intentions of the JWT: warring cannot be made a matter of honor or glory but must always be a matter of dealing justly with violence or oppression.
- Proportionality. The entire conflict, and particular engagements, must respect proportionality; that is, the war must not

cause more damage than that which it aims to prevent. The war should be proportional to the damage caused by the enemy.

- Respect for treaties and international law.
- Objectively, and for the JWT to make sense, only one side could be thought to fight "justly." However, each side may subjectively believe that they fight justly, and thus it is necessary to treat enemy combatants with the respect due them legally and as persons, assuming that they believe their cause to be just.

Jus in Bello

- Immunity of the innocent. Nonmilitants must not be targeted in war. "Innocent" means those who do not pose a threat and includes not only women, children, clergy, and unarmed men, but also soldiers taken prisoner. However, civilians may suffer harm if they remain in a besieged city or are close to military targets.
- Discrimination. Weapons must discriminate, that is, respect the immunity of the innocent. On this basis, weapons such as land mines—which still kill and maim decades later and show no judgment between old farmers or little boys and warring militants—have been argued by many to be a violation of the JWT. The same has been said of nuclear weapons. The same has been said by some about all "modern warfare."
- The methods used must be "necessary" or indispensable, the only possible way of getting to the stated aims of the engagement. This criterion, however, has been employed in two very different ways: necessity can be thought of as a lever of judgment *within* all the other rules; *or* necessity can be thought to legitimate *breaking* the other rules.
- The means should respect human dignity: no torture, slander, rape, or poisoning of wells; do keep truces and good faith, and give quarter to a combatant who surrenders.

The above is necessarily brief and representative, but it represents a tradition that, over many centuries, has developed a fundamental coherence, even though tensions and difficulties of interpretation necessarily arise.

But Do We Care?

The mainstream of the Western Christian tradition since the fourth century CE has claimed to adhere to something like the JWT. And there are many devoted Christians who have concluded that their faith requires something like it. Whether they are wrong or right, I suspect that the more troubling question is the one we are left asking Muslims who see war as justifiable when "justice" or "security" demands it; namely, what are we to make of the apparent ease with which such thinking becomes a tool of rationalization for whatever wars the nation has already decided to fight, or the ease with which the limiting rules have been so easily discarded or ignored? In teaching ethics courses, my agenda includes the criteria of the JWT. When I ask my students how many of them have ever heard a sermon or a Sunday school class on the criteria, twelve years of undergraduate teaching in a Christian university has yielded almost no affirmative responses.[9] So we might ask: if our preachers do not teach the criteria, if our Sunday school classes do not teach us the criteria, and if we do not know the criteria, how can we say we hold such beliefs? And if we are not firmly grounded in such moral restraints, what other sorts of rationalizations and logic are shaping us, molding us, deluding us?[10]

This brings us back to my home church in Alabama. All those issues of personal morality, taken so seriously, required effective means of character formation. For example, we took chastity seriously, and we heard (nigh unto) endless admonitions on the evils of lust. Self-restraint was a highly esteemed virtue, and the shepherds of the church did not wait until raging hormones led their little lambs to park cars on secluded streets and explore their adolescent fantasies. They taught us ahead of time because they knew the time of temptation would inevitably come. Moreover, in order not to fall prey to the wiles of lust, we were taught to embrace all sorts of other practices, such as abstinence from dancing and from "mixed bathing." If virginity was important, then accompanying practices had to be taught too. The practices we were taught may or may not have been effective. But the moral conviction had, at least, *integrity* in that the church community sought some means of character formation.

But the skills needed to ward off the amorous advances of the nationalists and the military-industrial complex are grossly lacking.

If we take chastity seriously, and we should, then it will not do to wait, to stand outside the car and knock at the fogged-over window when the boy is already on top of the girl. But do we not see this sort of practice in the American church with regard to the passion and lust that inevitably accompany warring?

Typically, "pacifism" is understood as "utopian" or "idealistic," while the JWT is construed as "realistic." Two notes in this regard: one, it is fundamentally flawed to see "pacifism" as an idealistic, rule-based ethic. "Genuine biblical pacifism," as Cahill notes, "does not revolve around the absolutization of any human values or rules, but around a converted life in Christ that subsumes and often changes every 'natural' pattern of behavior." In other words, one of the primary differences between the JWT and pacifism lies "in their disagreement about how present and accessible in human life the kingdom, by the grace of Christ, really is."[11]

Two, there are serious grounds for asking whether the JWT is "realistic" at all, in the sense that it can be used to limit the employment of violence. As Stanley Hauerwas recently noted, the very structure and commitments of nation-states make them unlikely candidates for adherents to the JWT.[12] The modern nation-state cannot envision itself as an entity willing to give its own life for another. The nation-state posits certain ideas, constructs, or "goods" for which everything must be "sacrificed," including the lives of those who happen, by mere historical accident, not to have been born within the nation-state's borders. The nation-state continues to live according to a sacrificial system, notes Hauerwas, which is willing to sacrifice our normal desire not to kill. We might say that though all sacrifice has been ended with the sacrifice of Christ, the modern nation-state has continued to insist that we practice child-sacrifice, the sacrifice of both our own young people and the babies of "enemy" nation-states.

While there are some remarkable exceptions, the history of Christianity demonstrates the many ways in which the fairly restrictive commitments of the Just War criteria have been co-opted, abused, and ignored in the heat and passion of war-making against whatever new enemy arose.

The Crusades are the most obvious place to begin illustrating that claim.

10

Crusading for Christ

> In Ma'arra our troops boiled pagan adults in cooking-pots; they impaled children on spits and devoured them grilled.
>
> —Frankish chronicler Radulph of Caen,
> describing the Crusaders' cannibalism

I lunched one day with my new Muslim acquaintance Mustafa at the American Colony Hotel in Jerusalem. As we visited, at one point he asked, "Did you know that in one of the Crusades the Christians *ate* the Muslims?" Had I not just read such an account a few days prior, I would not have believed him. But I had discovered some historical records that claimed this very thing, a historical anecdote that I do not recall ever having been taught in my seminary course on the history of Christianity. I replied with some shame, "I just recently read that."

The story is indeed so fantastic that it is difficult to believe. I would come across other stories that were repeated by more than one person in Palestine—for example, the claim that dissidents at the Council of Nicaea were put to death—for which I have found no historical evidence. But the cannibalism story is recounted by a Frankish chronicler and appears to be grounded in historical fact.[1]

But tales of Christian cannibalism are not the sort of tales that we Western Christians recount. We remember 9/11; we remember tales of the merciless Saracens; we remember the Alamo; we remember Pearl Harbor; but we do not cultivate in our collective vision the sorts of tales that cause us dis-ease with "our" injurious and unjust exploits. But "double vision" may require us to pay attention to the way others might tell the stories that we tell, or at least are vaguely familiar with, that justify our own sense of moral superiority. And thus Amin Maalouf's book *The Crusades through Arab Eyes*[2] serves as a helpful example; Maalouf tells the story not of "the Crusades," which is what they were in Western eyes. Instead, Maalouf wants to describe how the wars were experienced by the Arabs. The Arabs spoke instead "of Frankish wars, of 'the Frankish invasions.'"[3] So, Maalouf tells the tale of *the Franj*, relying almost exclusively upon Arabic historians and chroniclers.

The Franj killed and plundered their way across Palestine, on their way to Jerusalem. They laid siege upon the Syrian city of Ma'arra in 1098. The leaders of the city contacted Bohemond, the leader of the Crusaders. In exchange for their withdrawal from some buildings and the promise to stop fighting, Bohemond gave his word to preserve the life of the town's inhabitants—the same Bohemond who we noted earlier would send "to the Greek Emperor a whole cargo of noses and thumbs sliced from the Saracens."[4] Trusting Bohemond's promise, the families waited in fear for the Franj to arrive. And when the Franj arrived, Bohemond's promise was cast aside, and a slaughter ensued.

"For three days they put the people to the sword, killing more than a hundred thousand people and taking many prisoners,"[5] reported the Arabian chronicler Ibn al-Athīr. Maalouf notes that the

figures are obviously fantastic, for the city's population on the eve of its fall was probably less than ten thousand. But the horror lay less in the number of victims than in the barely imaginable fate that awaited them.

In Ma'arra our troops boiled pagan adults in cooking-pots; they impaled children on spits and devoured them grilled [reported the Frankish Christian chronicler Radulph of Caen]. The inhabitants of towns and villages near Ma'arra would never read this confession

. . . but they would never forget what they had seen and heard. The memory of these atrocities . . . shaped an image of the Franj that would not easily fade.[6]

The next year the Franj would take Jerusalem, on July 15, 1099, following a forty-day siege. The crusading Christians entered the city, heavily armored, and slaughtered men, women, and children. They plundered houses. They sacked the mosques. During the two days of killing, some Muslims slipped away in the chaos. Those who had remained in the city and survived until the last were forced to dump the bodies of their dead relatives in vacant lots and burn them. Then they were either sold into slavery or were themselves killed.[7]

The plight of the Jews in Jerusalem was no less horrid. The Jews had sought to defend their quarter of the city. When their defenses gave way and blond-headed knights poured into their streets, the Jews gathered at their synagogue to pray. The Franj blocked all exits, then ringed the building round with firewood and set it afire. Any who escaped the conflagration were killed in the alleyways, while the rest were burned.[8] Mallouf does not belabor the point, but it must continually be noted, I think: the Franj had come, of course, in the name of Jesus. As Saladin would say of these who came bearing the cross: "Regard the Franj! Behold with what obstinacy they fight for their religion, while we, the Muslims, show no enthusiasm for waging holy war."[9]

When the Franj had set out to recover Jerusalem from the hands of the Muslims, the Seljuk Turks had taken control of the Holy City, denying Western Christians admission to the holy sites.[10] When the Muslim emir of Cairo grew fearful of the Franj coming all the way to Jerusalem, he attacked Jerusalem preemptively, to free the city from the Seljuk Turks, and established a new policy, respecting the freedom of worship and the liberty of pilgrims to come to Jerusalem, provided they came unarmed and not in large groups. The Franks would hear none of it: "We will go all of us to Jerusalem, in combat formation, our lances raised."[11]

Ibn al-Athīr, writing approximately a century following the events, recounts that "the population of the holy city was put to the sword, and the Franj spent a week massacring Muslims. They killed more than seventy thousand people in al-Aqsā mosque." Maalouf, apparently unsure about Ibn al-Athīr's numbers, cites Ibn al-Qalānisi, "who never reported figures he could not verify, and says only: Many people were killed. The Jews had gathered in their synagogue and the Franj burned them alive. They also destroyed the monuments of saints and the tomb of Abraham, may peace be upon him!"[12]

The Franj also sacked the mosque of 'Umar, the caliph who was the second successor to Muhammad and who had conquered Jerusalem in 638. The irony for Christians is that "the Crusades" are typically and simply recounted as retaliation for Muslim offenses in Palestine. But again, it depends upon *which* Muslims one refers to (the Seljuk Turks, in this case, or the Muslims who had been living in the Middle East for centuries?). Moreover, Muslims want Christians to remember that the behavior of the Crusaders who reached Jerusalem in 1099 contrasts in disturbing ways with 'Umar's behavior, the first Muslim caliph who entered Jerusalem in 638. Maalouf recounts:

> The Arabs would later frequently invoke this event, to highlight the difference between their conduct and that of the Franj. 'Umar had entered Jerusalem astride his famous white camel, and the Greek patriarch of the holy city came forward to meet him. The caliph first assured him that the lives and property of the city's inhabitants would be respected, and then asked the patriarch to take him to visit the Christian holy places. The time of Muslim prayer arrived while they were in the church of Qiyāma, the Holy Sepulchre, and 'Umar asked his host if he could unroll his prayer mat. The patriarch invited 'Umar to do so right where he stood but the caliph answered: "If I do, the Muslims will want to appropriate this site, saying 'Umar prayed here.'" Then, carrying his prayer mat, he went and knelt outside. He was right, for it was on that very spot that the mosque that bore his name was constructed. The Frankish commanders, alas, lacked 'Umar's magnanimity. They celebrated their triumph with an ineffable orgy of killing, and then savagely ravaged the city they claimed to venerate.[13]

Moreover, the very name given to them by historians—Crusaders—arose from the fact that they wore a cloth cross on their clothes. Their "bearing of the cross" meant the slaughter of the inhabitants of the city where their alleged Lord had been persecuted instead of persecuting; had blessed, instead of cursed; had been killed, instead of killing.

Why the Crusades Are Not as Historically Irrelevant as We Might Think

"The Crusades" have spawned a cottage industry of academics who argue about precisely how we ought to define *crusade*, the genesis of the Crusades, and the varied motivations behind the Crusades. I cannot possibly sort all that out, for those who study the phenomena for an academic lifetime still have their arguments and unresolved hypotheses. Here, I simply wish to raise several observations that I think terribly important in our context.

First, please recollect the line of thinking that I have been developing here: the gospel is not a "religion," some compartment of one's private life that is separable from economics and politics and a way of life, configured either individually or communally. As I have noted already, this is a truth serious Muslims have not forgotten about their faith. And given that Muslims are not so prone to compartmentalize their faith as we Western Christians may be, then it makes sense that many Muslims could not help but look upon the churchgoing Western leaders (the Bushes, the Clintons, the Obamas, the Palins, and so forth) and conclude that the Christian West is waging war yet again upon Islam. So, note that one of Osama bin Laden's groups took the name "The World Islamic Front for Crusade against Jews and Crusaders."[14]

Surely, many of the jihadists overstate their case when they contend that imperialist expressions of liberalism are simply the new mask for the Crusades. But such a position is understandable and has been written into the consciousness of Muslims by high-profile, publicly professing Christians: after all, when General Allenby, representing the British Empire, took control of Jerusalem near the end of World War I, wresting it from the hands of the declining Ottoman Empire, he famously remarked that the Crusades were now over. And at the end of the century, when George W. Bush started the most recent war against Iraq in the name of the "war against terror," on presupposed justifications that all turned out to be false, he employed crusading language precisely in order to do so. "We will rid the world of the evil-doers," and "This crusade, this war on terrorism is gonna take awhile," and "This is a new kind of evil," said the Christian president.[15] All this language exhibits a fundamental misunderstanding of the historic restraints of the Just War tradition, leaving the West open to charges of "crusading."

Second, regardless of the precise historical factors—who did what first, and who was raping and pillaging and who was not—what is indisputable is that the Crusades did *not* arise out of a conflict between a community of Jesus disciples who were taking seriously the sociopolitical embodiment of nonviolent love of enemies, on the one hand, and a community of Muhammad disciples who were devoted to senseless slaughter on the other. The first Crusade against Jerusalem itself was initiated when Alexius I Comnenus, ruler of the Byzantine Empire in Constantinople, issued a call to Pope Urban II in the West for assistance in battling the ruthless and violent Turks. There were plenty of other Muslims in the Middle East—such as the emir of Cairo, who himself fought to free Jerusalem from the Turks—who desired a peaceable arrangement with Christian pilgrims. Comnenus had been hiring Western mercenaries for years to prop up his rule in Constantinople, and his control over Asia Minor, in his struggle with the Turks. Needing more help, he called upon Urban, who consented to the request by personally engaging himself in recruiting efforts, traveling throughout France to preach for the cause.[16]

While many such military missions were launched against the Muslims in the East, there were other objects in many other cases: the so-called Albigensian Crusades in 1209–29, launched against Christian heretics in southern France; the Baltic Crusades, waged periodically against pagan tribes from 1150 to 1400; the so-called Political Crusades, fought against enemies of the pope in Europe starting in the thirteenth century; and the Crusades provided opportunity for the persecution and killing of Jews in numerous instances.[17] War-making as a mechanism for bringing about "good"—once unleashed—found many outlets.

Who Defines the "Justice" for Which War Is Rightly Waged?

Note the claim made at some length by James Turner Johnson, that in the history of Christianity, crusading logic arose *from the JWT*: the "major normative tradition on war and statecraft in the West is not that of holy war but that of the just war. . . . The idea of the holy war developed as an element within the broader and more continuous tradition of the just war, but always in some tension with the content and direction of the broader tradition."[18] In other words, in a context in which there are Christian rulers, the question arises whether it is justifiable to wage war with regard to issues considered "religious." The Crusades were an affirmative answer to that question. Though often identified as a form of logic different than the JWT—and there are certainly legitimate cases that can be made along this line—the Crusades are consistent with the JWT in this regard. The Crusades issued from the conviction that freeing Jerusalem from the Seljuk Turks and guaranteeing pilgrims access to their holy sites were justified reasons for war. The formal logic is the same as the JWT's, and the same as Muhammad's logic on war: that under certain conditions, war is justifiable. In this particular case, the difference between Muhammad's logic and the Crusaders' logic was the difference in what conditions are legitimate criteria for engaging war.

But Christianity in Europe—especially in Constantinople—had gotten into bed with imperial power long ago, long before the invitation to the Crusades was issued. The Christian Charlemagne, king of the Franks, had determined some three centuries earlier to either baptize or kill the pagan Saxons, which he did quite effectively. Moreover, he was not scolded for his policy by the papacy but rather crowned emperor of the Holy Roman Empire. No doubt there were power struggles between the papacy and the emperor—as the very tale of Charlemagne's coronation sufficiently attests. But this is precisely the point: it was a grasping after power that could "make things turn out right," we might say. It was a struggle to wield the power of imperial might—either directly or indirectly—on behalf of what the supposed good guys thought was good. This is not to say that such rulers ignored justice or that all employed violence capriciously. But they were nonetheless a long distance from the early church fathers, who had refused to practice this way of wielding power.

And though we often arrogantly think—especially in our looking down our noses at Muslims—that we are a long way from such medieval thinking, those medieval habits of thought continue in the church today, as we shall see.

11

The Cowboy Museum

Thus was God pleased to smite our enemies, and to give us their Land for an Inheritance.

—Captain John Mason, celebrating the killing of Pequot Indian men, women, and children

The recollection of a childhood memory drew me to the National Cowboy and Western Heritage Museum in Oklahoma City some while back. When I was a child, my family had toured the museum on a vacation "out West," probably some thirty years ago. I remembered only this one image from the museum: the larger-than-life sculpture by famed artist James Earle Fraser titled *End of the Trail*. The sculpture portrays a dejected and defeated Cherokee warrior upon his mighty horse of war—the magnificent horse, too, in a posture of defeat, consequent to the white man's coming. Fraser's work memorializes Andrew Jackson's forced relocation of the Cherokee westward.[1]

Along with my vague childhood memory of the sculpture was another recollection: my father's sense of sadness, and his few words of lamentation uttered in response to this monument to injustice.

I'd had, as I recall it, enough grammar school to understand that several tribes of Native Americans had once populated the region now called Alabama. Geography and names and historical monuments reminded me, as a boy, that *my* people were the newcomers to this place. I was raised in the hills around Talladega, Alabama. Talladega was the name of a Creek Indian village, and in our county was Mount Cheaha, the highest geographical point in the state. *Cheaha*, according to some sources, means "high place" in the Creek language. So this sculpture said to me, even as a child, something like this: other people once lived in the Alabama hills you love; other people once walked amid the long-leaf pines; other people once loved the red clay of the place you call home. The beginning of the Trail of Tears began in the Southeast that I called home, and I was not quite sure how to process that.

So, I wanted to see that sculpture again. The Cowboy Museum does depict Native American culture, I thought, in a compelling and beautiful manner. Nevertheless, these artifacts sit uneasily alongside the celebration of cowboy culture. After all, Dee Brown teaches us that all the "great myths of the American West"—"tales of fur traders, mountain men, steamboat pilots, goldseekers, gamblers, gunmen, cavalrymen, cowboys, harlots, missionaries, schoolmarms, and homesteaders"—arose out of the very same forces by which "the culture and civilization of the American Indian was destroyed."[2] And sure enough, I found in the museum no placard that says, "Look at the violence of it all; look at the manner in which Protestant Christianity supported and gave warrant for the conquest of this land; look at the injustice waged, all in the name of progress, Manifest Destiny, and the will of God." The museum simply seems to assume that Native American artifacts can sit quietly alongside the display of firearms, the magnificent display of Colts and Winchesters, the display of "how the West was won."

Taking Stock

Before proceeding with a tale of "how the West was won," allow me to review some ground we have covered: Muhammad begins, under persecution in Mecca, with a policy of nonretaliation. But after the emigration to Medina, he adopts a policy of measured retaliation in response to aggression. The war-making is not employed for the sake of "religion" as such but for the sake of justice and security—the understanding of which is informed by Islam.

Following the death of Muhammad, two Islamic dynasties expand the dominion of Muslim culture and faith, developing an understanding and practice of war that is interwoven with imperial power. And I raise the question: though the classic statements on war in the classical era of Islam speak in categories similar to the Christian Just War tradition, is there not here a slippery slope in which the circumstances that are thought to justify war may become increasingly broad?

In the Christian tradition, the founding narrative of Jesus advocates and employs nonretaliatory love of enemies, and Jesus is persecuted unto death. Vindicated in resurrection, the early church also embraced nonretaliatory love of enemies, rejecting warfare as legitimate for disciples of Jesus. But when the Roman Empire begins to embrace the Christian church, a new ethic develops: the Just War tradition. For these early JWT thinkers, war was regrettable and a horrific necessity in the midst of a world that remains marred by sin.

But once this new logic is embraced, that war is justifiable under certain conditions, and once the Christian church allies itself with the imperial powers, we find the justification of war and violence growing more and more lax. Charlemagne's war policy—either be baptized or we will kill you—and in time the rise of the Crusades both serve as examples. More and more conditions are seen as justifying the making of war.

Here is the next major observation that seems important to make. We think we've come such a long way from the Crusades, that the Enlightenment freed the West from the dangerous mix of "religion and violence," and that we good Western Christians are unlike the premodern Muslims and have moved beyond the Christian medieval mistakes.

Because we have sought in the West (for the good, I think) to separate church and state, and because the experiment we call the United States was grounded upon the assumed good (and indeed good, I think) of the free exercise of religion, we also assume that we are not prone to any of the dangers of fanatical war-making of which we suspect Muslims. But *perhaps* these moves in the West have not made us any less prone to fanatical war-making. *Perhaps* the old logic of "war is bad but justified under certain conditions" has simply expanded to fit the conviction that the US must be preserved at all costs. And perhaps the well-intentioned Just War theorists are quite correct that we are particularly prone to ignore the rules for what is legitimate to do *in* war.

Our Christian Forebears upon the Eastern Shores

As numerous writers have made clear, the beginning of the trail westward began in a manner as ugly as its end. The Puritans, recently arrived from England, soon found themselves in competition for land with its original inhabitants. The Puritans, in short order, had their own tales to tell that justified in their minds vengeful war-making. A dozen or so Indians had killed an apparently contentious white man named John Oldham. He was found with his head cut open all the way to his brains, and with his legs almost cut off. A man named John Gallop came upon the scene of the murder and in response killed a dozen or so Indians.[3] After taking one Indian captive, binding him with ropes, Gallop took another and bound him similarly. Ill at ease due to the stories he had heard of Indians being capable of untying themselves when kept together in captivity, Gallop took the latter captive and threw him, still bound, into the sea.

But the death of some dozen or so Native Americans in retribution for the one white man was apparently not vengeance enough. Thus, Captain John Underhill declared that "the blood of the innocent called for vengeance." Underhill set out from Boston in August of 1636 under the leadership of Captain John Endicott to deliver such vengeance. Landing at Block Island, Endicott and his men hunted for two days for Indians to either capture or kill. According to the surviving eyewitness account, they did not kill all the men on the island only because of "the Indians being retired into swamps, so as we could not find them. We burnt and spoiled both houses and corn in great abundance; but they kept themselves in obscurity." Thus, on day one of their foray, the Englishmen busied themselves "burning and spoiling the island," continuing such destruction the second day. Historian Richard Drinnon

85

continues, "In all they burned the wigwams of two villages, threw Indian mats on and burned 'great heaps of pleasant corn ready shelled,' 'destroyed some of their dogs instead of men,' and staved in canoes."[4] Endicott continued on his way from Block Island to confront the Pequots the next day. When they offered to parley unarmed, Captain Endicott preferred to "bid them battle." The Pequots would not engage the battle, so Endicott spent that day, again, "burning and spoiling the country." Sailing that night to Narragansett Bay, the English found that the Indians again would not engage the battle, so they "burnt and spoiled what [they] could light on."[5]

As I was recounting such tales recently, a fellow church member replied, "But the Indians were not always peaceable—they could be very violent." No doubt—and this is beside the point. The more important concern, I replied, is that the Spanish conquistadores bashed babies' heads, and the Puritans slaughtered Native Americans in the name of Jesus, in celebration that they were bringing the gospel to these shores.

Indeed, when Captain John Mason subsequently took up the war against the Pequots, he believed his work mandated by God: "The Lord was as it were pleased to say unto us, The Land of Canaan will I give unto thee though but few and Strangers in it." Similarly, the Reverend Thomas Hooker had prophesied that the Pequots should be so defeated "that they should be Bread for us."[6] So Mason and his fellow soldiers launched a surprise attack against the Pequots' fort on June 5, 1637, before dawn. The men, women, and children still slept, and the soldiers began to burn the fort. Drinnon recounts: "The stench of frying flesh, the flames, and the heat drove the English outside the walls." John Underhill, fighting along with Mason, recounted that many of the Pequots "were burnt in the fort, both men, women, and children. Others [who were] forced out . . . our soldiers received and entertained with the point of the sword. Down fell men, women, and children."[7] So the war against the Pequots quickly moved from burning corn and wigwams to the burning of four hundred men, women, and children, in the space of one hour.

Mason and Underhill rejoiced, convinced that their merciless triumph was the work of God, indeed that God "had fitted the hearts of men for the service." Underhill was later asked by other Indian tribesmen, "Why should you be so furious?" He referred them to the

Scriptures: "When a people is grown to such a height of blood, and sin against God and man, and all the confederates in the action, there he hath no respect to persons, but harrows them, and saws them, and puts them to the sword, and the most terriblest death that may be." In other words, Underhill summarized: "We had sufficient light from the word of God for our proceedings."[8]

A few weeks later, Captain Israel Stoughton arrived with more militiamen and captured a hundred Pequot refugees who were hiding in a swamp. According to one Puritan observer, some twenty of those captured were taken by John Gallop to "feed the fishes with 'em," that is, to throw the still-bound captives into the sea. Stoughton hunted down other Pequot families who the pursuers knew could travel only slowly because of their children. Drinnon recounts that "three hundred of the quarry were literally run to ground. Many of those killed were tramped into the mud or buried in swamp mire."[9]

Reflecting upon the Pequot War, Captain John Mason concluded: "Thus was God pleased to smite our enemies, and to give us their Land for an Inheritance."[10] Mason received fame and fortune and was appointed major general of the Connecticut militia. In ceremonial fashion, Reverend Hooker gave Mason a staff "like an ancient Prophet addressing himself to the Military Officer," reported an observer. The staff was given to Mason as "the Principal Ensign of Martial Power, to Lead the Armies and Fight the Battles of the Lord and of his People," reported Thomas Prince.[11]

Such tales could be multiplied many times over in American history, in which Christian faith, combined with a deep trust in the goodness of the cause of "America," went forth to wage merciless battle and legitimated its own tyranny in the name of its own self-righteous crusade. The enslavement of Africans, the war for Texas, the wrenching of California from Mexico, and the slaughter and disenfranchisement of Native Americans were often accompanied by an admixture of God and country.

Our Christian Forebears beyond the Western Shores

Having conquered from sea to shining sea, the US sought to expand westward into the Pacific, a move described in painful detail by James

87

Bradley in his book *Flyboys*. Having committed its grotesque "rape of China"—no one knows how many were raped, tortured, and slaughtered, but some estimate thirty million deaths—Japan found itself the object of well-justified international derision. The US and Britain would both denounce Japan's bombing of Nanking, China, and officials would call such bombing "barbarous" and a violation of "principles of law and humanity."[12] Alas, both Britain and the US would bomb many cities in such fashion within less than a decade.

Bradley notes that the Japanese leaders saw themselves doing to China only what the Americans had previously done to the American Indians and the Mexicans and the Filipinos. Bradley comments, "To the Japanese, the depth of the western Christians' hypocrisy was breathtaking. Japan was taming her own Wild West as the Americans had theirs."[13] Teddy Roosevelt—memorialized at Mount Rushmore, which stands on land stolen from Native Americans, where a bronze plaque commemorates that "progressive, adventurous Americans spread civilization and Christianity"—had "relished the chance to bring Christian civilization to America's first major colonial possession in the Pacific."[14]

The US entered the fray in the Philippines under the pretext of responding to the abuses and tyranny of Spain against the Filipino freedom fighters. But the US exceeded the inhumanity it purported to rectify. More than 250,000 Filipino men, women, and children were killed, in the name of bringing civilization and Christianity—some 7,000 per month. Most of these were civilians. A policy of taking no prisoners of war meant instead the policy of slaughtering the population. The tale is a sorry one. One American captain described "one of the prettiest little towns we have passed through," where the civilians there desired peace with the Americans and "stood along the side of the road, took off their hats, touched their foreheads with their hands. 'Buenos Dias, Senors' (means good morning)," and then the soldier boys proceeded to kill the residents and destroy the village.

Another soldier wrote that "we bombarded a place called Malabon, and then we went in and killed every native we met, men, women and children," while another said that the fun of killing civilians was a "'hot game,' and beats rabbit hunting all to pieces. We charged them and such a slaughter you never saw. We killed them like rabbits; hundreds, yes thousands of them. Everyone was crazy."

A general demanded that no POWs be taken: "I want no prisoners. I wish you to kill and burn, the more you kill and burn the better it will please me." A New York soldier wrote about the massacre in a town called Titatia, "I am probably growing hard-hearted, for I am in my glory when I can sight my gun on some dark skin and pull the trigger. Tell all my inquiring friends that I am doing everything I can for Old Glory and for America I love so well."[15] President Roosevelt would declare the war in the Philippines the "most glorious war in the nation's history."[16]

Christians in America are too poorly informed of these tales. We would rather have feel-good, patriotic piety-fests on the Sunday before Memorial Day. On those Sundays we equate "Greater love hath no man than this, that a man lay down his life for his friends" with the killing and dying of "our" soldiers, all the while ignoring the plain fact that the "greater love" described in 1 John was the voluntary, loving act of dying at the hands of one's enemies, instead of the act of dying while seeking to kill one's enemies. We would do better, I think, to read Mark Twain's "War Prayer" in church. We would do better to cite in our churches these words of General George Patton: "No one ever won a war by dying for their country. They won by making the other son-of-a-bitch die for his."[17] Of course, we good Christians will not cite George Patton because of the profane language, but we celebrate Patton's method all the same.

12

The Western Tradition of Terror

War is hell.

—Attributed to William Tecumseh
Sherman, Union general
in the American Civil War

After a lecture to the Nashville Chapter of the United Nations Association in which I had discussed some of the similarities and differences between the Christian and Islamic traditions on war and peacemaking, an elderly man stood and said that he had been an airman in World War II, a navigator who flew over Japan soon after the dropping of "the bomb." "I will never be able to forget what I saw," he said. "We killed 186,000 people in an instant with the bomb. What does your 'Just War tradition' have to say about that?"[1] "If one takes all the criteria of the Just War tradition seriously," I replied, "then the tradition can only say that the dropping of the bomb was immoral." He nodded his head in sad satisfaction with my answer and sat down.

Some minutes later, an elderly, silver-haired woman, sporting a knitted, hot-pink hat, raised her hand. She began in a pleasant voice: "You probably remember the story of Noah, and when God got so angry that he wiped everyone out?" "Yes," I said. Her voice gradually grew more tense, "And you said the dropping of the bomb was immoral?" "Yes," I said. "Well," she replied, "I thank God for Harry Truman dropping the bomb, and when I think about the Japanese and the Bataan marches, I just wish I could get my hands on some of those Japanese" —and she began a ripping and strangling motion, voice angry—"and I think when you get a little older, you'll get a little wiser and think differently."

On Possibly (but Perhaps Necessarily) Belaboring a Point

At this point in my storytelling, one might object, "Enough already! Why more horrific storytelling?" Here is one reason: the stories we tell determine the ethic from which we live and from which we see the world. And if the fundamental story we Western Christians tell ourselves is the tale of an ever-righteous, God-fearing nation triumphing over the forces of evil through the power of military might, we will be tempted to jump on the nationalist bandwagon the next time the drums of war are beaten.

A second reason: the unfolding story of war-making by the US is the unfolding story of war no longer governed by restraint. The absolute belief in the necessity of winning at any and every cost is not only a denial of the historic restraints found in both Muhammad and Augustine but also something more pernicious: the idolatrous conviction that our survival is more important than any other value.

World War II is commonly called "the good war." Conventional wisdom has it that it was a "good war" because the reason for going to war was so obviously justified. But some Just War theorists have noted that the rules for what is legitimate to do *in war* were in many cases ignored because of the strong conviction in the rightness of the cause. Thus, the war stands as a marker in which we, on a widespread basis, began to believe that everything is justified in war: something called "total war."

The Birth of "Total War"

Daniel Bell notes that "the U.S. Civil War is generally recognized as the real watershed in the birth of 'total war.'"[2] That is, the United

States bequeathed to the world a new form of war, in which restraints that had historically limited the destruction and loss of life of civilians were now seen as increasingly infeasible, for "war is hell." Such was, William Tecumseh Sherman's logic as he burned his way across the South in the midst of the American Civil War. It was reported by an observer that Sherman, upon being upbraided by a Nashvillian for his soldiers' behavior on a march to Knoxville, replied: "War is cruelty. There is no use trying to reform it, the crueler it is, the sooner it will be over."[3] And that cruelty and harshness, visited upon the women and children of the South, was seen as the means to bring about peace.[4] The war was a battle between two societies, and thus the entire populace could rightly be made to suffer. Commenting upon the "dress rehearsal" for his destructive march to the sea, Sherman noted that the destruction of Meridian, Mississippi, was preparatory to "make this war as severe as possible and make no symptoms of [being] tire[d], till the South begs for mercy."[5]

"Total War" and the "Good War"

Consequently, the *rhetoric* of "just war" gets cast about, justifying and rationalizing all sorts of immoral behavior, while the traditional restraints are cast aside. World War II was justified, one can rightly say, according to the JWT rules for going *to* war, but the rules for restraint *in* war were cast aside, as a promiscuous man hides his wedding band on the way to the whorehouse. Hamburg, for example, was firebombed in the midst of an extended heat wave in the summer of 1943. The Royal Air Force, in conjunction with the US Eighth Army Air Force, initiated Operation Gomorrah, attempting to reduce the city to rubble and ashes. Starting at 1:00 a.m. on July 27, the raid dropped ten thousand tons of bombs on a thickly populated area of homes. High-explosive bombs first ripped doors and windows apart. Incendiary bombs started fires on the rooftops. Heavier firebombs fell into lower stories of the homes. The huge fires quickly converged so that the entire area was engulfed in flames. By 1:20 a.m., the firestorm raged with such intensity that it rose two thousand meters skyward, ferociously sucking oxygen so that the winds feeding the fire reached hurricane velocity, "resonating like mighty organs with all their stops pulled out at once." For three hours the fire consumed like this, tearing roofs and gables from buildings, flinging rafters, and uprooting trees, while it "drove human beings before it like living torches." The fire rolled "like a tidal wave through the streets," melting glass in tramcars, setting to boil sugar in the cellars of bakeries. "Those who had fled from their air-raid shelters sank, with grotesque contortions, in the thick bubbles thrown up by the melting asphalt."[6]

Disfigured corpses were strewn everywhere. "Bluish little phosphorous flames still flickered around many of them; others had been roasted brown or purple and reduced to a third of their normal size. They lay doubled up in pools of their own melted fat, which had sometimes already congealed." When work crews entered in August, they found that "clumps of flesh and bone or whole heaps of bodies had cooked in the water gushing from bursting boilers. Other victims had been so badly charred and reduced to ashes by the heat . . . that the remains of families consisting of several people could be carried away in a single laundry basket."[7]

The rats gorged and fattened upon corpses; maggots as long as a finger covered cellar floors; flies copulated and consumed, satiated from the waste, "huge and iridescent green."[8] Like a horror story, and yet purposefully planned and executed by the Allies. A purposed aftermath of homelessness: one and a quarter million refugees from Hamburg, dispersed in every direction. Friedrich Reck, in his diary entry dated August 20, 1943, described a group of refugees forcing their way toward a train in Bavaria, when a cardboard suitcase "falls on the platform, bursts open and spills its contents. Toys, a manicure case, singed underwear. And last of all, the roasted corpse of a child, shrunk like a mummy, which its half-deranged mother had been carrying about with her, the relic of a past that was still intact a few days ago."[9]

In such fashion W. G. Sebald recounts the firebombing of the cities of Germany. England sat secluded on its isle in 1941, unable to enter the war as Nazi Germany had swept across Europe, ready to enter Africa and Asia.[10] The strategy devised was a system of widespread bombing of cities, intentionally targeting domestic and residential areas. Though the campaign was hotly debated, the government finally set out upon the policy, mobilizing industrial processes and amassing weaponry, bombers, and pilots precisely for the purpose of bombing the German civilian population.

Like an echo of Sherman's strategy, the British government's goal was "to destroy the morale of the enemy civilian population and, in particular, of the industrial workers."[11] This is, through and through, the tactic of terror: seeking to achieve one's goal of defeating the enemy by targeting the morale of the civilian population. Critics would later point out that the Royal Air Force could have, in fact, targeted industrial factories, which would have, as the Nazi architect Albert Speer indicated in his memoirs, quickly paralyzed Germany's system of production. Sebald notes that the many young British boys-turned-bombers were co-opted into a game of Russian roulette in which sixty out of a hundred lost their lives, and that according to one estimate, as much as one-third of Britain's war material was dedicated to the aerial bombing campaigns.[12] Though Churchill expressed scruples against the wholesale destruction of cities and civilians, he believed a higher justice to be at work, "that those who have loosed these horrors upon mankind will now in their homes and persons feel the shattering strokes of just retribution."[13] And, as we will see shortly, this logic of the westernized, civilized, Christian Churchill is the same logic employed half a century later by the Muslim Osama bin Laden. The British and the Americans simply had more industrial capacity at hand and thus were able to burn and slaughter more civilians than bin Laden has been able to, as of yet—and may God grant mercy that bin Laden *not* acquire the same capacity the Christian Americans and British and Germans acquired in the middle of the twentieth century.

Though it became clear that the campaign failed to affect the morale of the German populace, and though more effective strategies were available to the British military toward the goal of paralyzing Germany's military-industrial complex, the widespread slaughter continued unabated. In time, the Royal Air Force dropped more than one million tons of bombs in attacking 131 cities and towns, many of which were, Sebald reports, "almost entirely flattened," killing around six hundred thousand civilians and destroying three and a half million homes.[14]

And this does not begin to get at the Americans doing the very same thing to many Japanese cities, over and over again. In the recent documentary *Fog of War*, Robert McNamara rhetorically asks of Curtis LeMay's Japanese firebombing campaign: "Should you kill one hundred thousand people in one night, by firebombing or any other way? LeMay's answer would be clearly, 'Yes.'"[15] The massive firebombing campaign killed more civilians than did the dropping of the atom bombs on Hiroshima and Nagasaki. It is of the utmost politically incorrect stance to even question "the greatest generation" about World War II, because the reason for entering the war was to stop such horrible injustice. The cult of Japanese militarism that grew into an insidious manifestation of the early twentieth century was, no doubt, perverse beyond description. And the insidious manifestation of patriotic nationalism in the Nazis was, no doubt, perverse beyond description. Those stories have been told, and should be told and retold, as a lesson to us all. These stories do, in fact, portray well the sort of wickedness that the Genesis account of Noah was getting at: a vile affliction, which cries out to heaven for redress. But this does not change the fact that America and her allies did not fight the war according to the other commitments of the Just War tradition, and in this way, the war was not justifiable if we take the JWT seriously. Some may object that the Allies may have never won the war if they had fought according to the rules. This may or may not be true. But the fact that this objection carries so much weight makes the very point I am concerned with: that we do not, on the whole, take the JWT seriously. There are other powers at work, other forms of logic at work, a sacredness that blesses our war-making, rather than the hard work of discerning whether our warring fits the constraints of the JWT.

We like the JWT's formal logic—that war can be justified—but we do not like its constraints. Otherwise, why would a friend of mine, a lifelong Christian with a doctoral degree in spiritual development, crack the joke about "just drop the bomb and let God sort it out"? Why would almost all the leaders of the various mainline denominations, as well as the Catholic bishops, counsel that one of our recent wars did not fit the criteria of the tradition, but our churches bless our soldiers as they are paraded off to the war?[16] We are like addicts, war addicts, who are unaware of our powerlessness, and while thus unaware, there is little hope for recovery. Meanwhile, we go to church and sing pious songs and pray for "our soldiers" (as if, like Benedict who called monks to wage war in Jerusalem, we believe the church to have soldiers), and thus assume that our war-making and firebombing and destruction of water systems is quite legitimate because we feel good about our personal relationship with God. This is not merely an argument about pacifism. This is about the fact that the church ignores the JWT too. This is about the move toward "total war," in which we are told we must wage merciless war on behalf of the good news of democracy and free-market economies and political liberalism so we might be free to worship the Lord who in Jesus taught us to love our enemies.

Good God, have mercy on us.

13

Terrorism bin Laden Style

If we are attacked, then we have the right to attack back. Whoever has destroyed our villages and towns, then we have the right to destroy their villages and towns. Whoever has stolen our wealth, then we have the right to destroy their economy. And whoever has killed our civilians, then we have the right to kill theirs.

—Osama bin Laden[1]

On "Moral Equivalency"

By this point, I expect that some will accuse me of "moral equivalency." That is, some may be thinking that I am justifying Muslim terror atrocities by comparing them to Christian incidents of terror and unrestrained war-making. But as I clearly stated, I intend no rationalizing or excusing or justifying on anyone's part. My concern instead is that we practice honest self-examination rather than the dishonest procedure of comparing an idealized form of our faith tradition with the messy historical record of Muslims.

Moreover, to compare one's deeds with another's deeds for the purpose of justifying one's deeds is precisely what I am arguing *against*. This sort of reasoning has eaten away at the restraints of the Just War tradition. The Nazis immorally firebombed civilians in London, much to the protest and indignation of the British people; in time, the British would do the same to the German civilians. The Japanese, as we saw previously, believed their inhumanity to the Chinese was legitimated by what the Americans had done to the Native Americans; the British and Americans denounced the Japanese bombing of Nanking; and the Japanese, of course, launched a sneak attack upon the American military at Pearl Harbor. The rightful offense at such attacks would, in time, give rise to the Americans acting similarly toward the Japanese, burning and bombing their cities.

Our exercise here, then, is in fact not an exercise in "moral equivalency" for the sake of excusing any sort of terrorist behavior. It is, in fact, precisely an argument *against* such logic, which is used so very often on both sides of a conflict. And it is, in fact, the sort of logic that Osama bin Laden has employed to justify his own horrific efforts at slaughtering civilians.

Bin Laden's "Moral Equivalency"

Bin Laden justifies his mass murder by way of the claim that the United States has exempted itself from the rules—the rules regarding torture, the rules regarding the protection of nonmilitants in war, the rules regarding being subject to trial for war crimes. Bin Laden's killing of civilians and sowing of terror is immoral, despicable, and a horrid exercise in mass murder. But if Christian love calls us to the hard work of love of enemies, then that love of enemy surely requires, at least, that we listen to what that one is trying to say, requires the "double vision" that seeks to put ourselves in the other's shoes. This does not justify the wrongs; it merely asks what we may need to learn about ourselves, in the midst of this seemingly intractable cycle of violence.

The tale of Osama bin Laden: a son of privilege, from a multi-billionaire family with the highest connections in Saudi Arabia, university-educated, wealthy, quiet, tall, and serious—thence to caves in Afghanistan where he was hunted by the most powerful military on the face of the earth. Born in 1957 in Saudi Arabia, bin Laden was the seventeenth of fifty-two children. His father immigrated as a poor laborer to Saudi Arabia from Yemen and grew a small construction company into one of the largest in the Middle East, with a subsequent "industrial and financial empire."[2] In one of the many ironies of the tale of the US and Osama bin Laden, the Bin Laden Group built many of the military bases in Saudi Arabia, including bases employed by the US military, though it is precisely the presence of the US military that has been one of bin Laden's primary points of contention with the West.

Though bin Laden is considered US Public Enemy Number One, a deep irony lies here, for bin Laden regularly voices the logic employed in much Western thought on war-making. He chooses terminology that would not be thought politically correct by many in the West (you will find no hesitation in bin Laden's use of the word *terror*), but the formal *logic* may be found on the lips of many an American Christian politician. For example, in an interview some years prior to the 9/11 attacks, bin Laden asserted that "terrorism" is of two types: the "commendable" and the "reprehensible." To terrify the innocent is

> objectionable and unjust. . . . Whereas, terrorizing oppressors and criminals and thieves and robbers is necessary for the safety of people and for the protection of their property. . . . [E]very state and every civilization and culture has to resort to terrorism under certain circumstances for the purpose of abolishing tyranny and corruption. . . . [Armies, police forces, security forces are] all designed to terrorize whoever even contemplates to attack that country or its citizens. The terrorism we practice is of the commendable kind for it is directed at the tyrants and the aggressors and the enemies of Allah. . . . [T]errorizing those and punishing them are necessary measures to straighten things and to make them right.[3]

In this way bin Laden's "good terror" parallels the very notion of "shock and awe" that has governed much of the recent war campaign in the Middle East. And it parallels the "myth of redemptive violence" so pervasive in Hollywood's depiction of the conflict between good and evil. What would the stock characters played by Clint Eastwood and Mel Gibson be without the very logic articulated by bin Laden?

Of course, Westerners will object that bin Laden does not separate the call for avenging of wrongs through war from the call for all humanity to accept Islam. But suffice it here to say that to practice double vision will require a thought experiment something like this: imagine an American saying that he is willing to fight a war against an aggressor; imagine that this aggressor has inflicted great harm upon a third party of civilians; and imagine that in fighting the war, the American calls upon his defeated enemy to accept democracy. In this scenario, the American simply says he will fight on behalf of justice and democracy—that is, *fight on behalf of justice, defined in terms of what he believes to be most important*. Bin Laden, in this respect, is saying the same thing. What he believes to be most important is God and God's will. What the American, in our thought experiment, believes to be most important is democracy. And both are willing to wage war against their opponents on behalf of what they believe to be most important.

Bin Laden's Rationale for Targeting Civilians

As we have seen, both the early Islamic teaching and the early Christian Just War tradition set limits upon who is a legitimate target of war-making. And just as the American Civil War and World War II saw the erosion of the protection of nonmilitants, so it is with bin Laden. Prior to September 11, 2001, bin Laden maintained he was fighting against the US government and *not* the US people. But even so, since the US is a democracy, bin Laden contends, Americans are responsible for the deeds of their government. Western peoples must not only be grieved by the sight of "our children being killed in Israeli raids launched by American planes," he argues; "what they ought to do is change their governments which attack our countries." While the Western governments bear the blame, says bin Laden, for the injustices leveled upon Muslims, the citizenry must take heed: "If their people do not wish to be harmed inside their very own countries, they should seek to elect governments that are truly representative of them and that can protect their interests."[4]

Bin Laden makes this logic explicit following 9/11 in his "Letter to America": a democratic citizenry bears the weight of the responsibility for its leaders and its leaders' injustices. Bin Laden takes the claim of democratic freedom as the assertion of direct responsibility of the citizenry for the actions of its leaders: you elected them, they act on your behalf, and if they commit crimes against us, then you who elected them are responsible. "Thus the American people have chosen, consented to, and affirmed their support for the Israeli oppression of the Palestinians . . . and its continuous killing, torture, punishment and expulsion of the Palestinians." That bin Laden genuinely cares about the plight of the Palestinians I am not convinced. It seems to me to be an open question whether the Arab nations generally care more for the plight of individual Palestinians or more for the rhetorical value of the Palestinian plight. But in any case, bin Laden's rationale runs thus: American taxpayers fund the bombers and tanks and armies. American citizens constitute the army itself. In other words, bin Laden maintains that there are no "innocents" in America: "The American people cannot be . . . innocent of all the crimes committed by the Americans and Jews against us."[5]

Bin Laden's logic here—holding a citizenry as a whole responsible, and thus blameworthy, and thus legitimate targets of the pain of war—gives rise to a complete disregard for many of the historic protections accorded noncombatants in war. But again, this logic is not foreign to the American war experience, as evidenced in William Tecumseh Sherman's making the South "beg for mercy," in Churchill's bombing of civilians, and in the nuclear obliteration of Hiroshima and Nagasaki.

While bin Laden's hatred of and mass killing of US civilians purports to arise from US offenses, his hatred of Jews appears more inherent in his convictions. Thus, "the Jews" receive special place alongside "the Americans." It is America and the Jews, bin Laden contends, that have mobilized against Muslims. "The truth is that the whole Muslim world is the victim of international terrorism, engineered by Americans at the United Nations." Americans and Jews represent "the spearhead with which the members of our religion have been slaughtered. Any effort directed against America and the Jews yields positive and direct results—Allah willing. It is far better for anyone to kill a single American soldier than to squander his efforts on other activities."[6] Bin Laden justifies such bigotry and hatred by appealing to a long historic tradition: "The enmity between us and the Jews goes far back in time and is deep rooted. There is no question that war between the two of us is inevitable."[7]

And in apocalyptic arrogance, bin Laden claims that just as the mujahideen defeated the Soviets in Afghanistan in a decade-long war in the 1980s, the fighters would, "with the grace of Allah—prevail over the Americans and over the Jews, as the Messenger of Allah promised us in an authentic prophetic tradition when He said the Hour of Resurrection shall not come before Muslims fight Jews and before Jews hide behind trees and behind rocks."[8]

Most simply put, the logic of bin Laden runs thus: "Allah, the Almighty, legislated the permission and the option to take revenge. Thus, if we are attacked, then we have the right to attack back. Whoever has destroyed our villages and towns, then we have the right to destroy their villages and towns. Whoever has stolen our wealth, then we have the right to destroy their economy. And whoever has killed our civilians, then we have the right to kill theirs."[9]

14

Taking Stock

Perhaps a bit of summarizing is in order, given the progress of the inquiry. The following are the fundamental observations that I think are most important to take away and which I think are being said too little.

1. The founding narratives of Christianity and Islam are different.

In my experience, it is typical on the one hand for many who are fearful of Islam to rush to claim that Islam celebrates war-making and Christianity celebrates peacemaking. On the other hand, those who distance themselves from such fearmongering often rush with open arms to claim that there is "no difference" between Christianity and Islam, that both are simply manifestations of the same basic root religious impulse, a desire for peace and love of neighbor.

I think both of these inclinations are wrong.

Christianity and Islam *do* proceed from two very different narratives. These different stories carry profound implications for the question at hand. The founding narrative of Christianity is grounded in a suffering Messiah. Recollect that *Messiah* is synonymous with *King*. And this King came as all good kings come, to establish justice and righteousness, a just social order; to put it negatively, this King came to deal with and confront injustice and violence and the oppression of human history—what we churchgoers call sin. And this King did so through the teaching and practice of suffering love. As much sociological and historical research continues to show, Jesus chose a method of nonretaliatory love. He did *not* choose to be *passive*. But he also did not choose to take up the way of armed revolution, though there were other messianic claimants who did precisely that in the first century. Jesus spoke the truth to the powers, called for social change—such as forgiveness of debts, the practice of reconciliation, the breaking down of marginalizing taboos, and the love of enemies—and consequently, he was crucified. Crucifixion was the imperial power's way of humiliating and shaming anyone who dared challenge its political might. Jesus's followers subsequently proclaimed that Jesus had been resurrected from the dead, which is a way of saying that God vindicated *this way* of overcoming the powers of oppression, the "power of sin."

This was itself a new "politics," a new way of organizing a community, a community that would be called "church," which sought to embody this politics in its life together. As Jesus had suffered at the hands of the authorities, so did the church in time, trusting that the power of resurrection that had vindicated Jesus would vindicate Jesus's followers too should they have to suffer the fate of martyrdom.

The founding story of Islam begins in a similar way. When Muhammad begins to recite the Qur'an, his message is a sociopolitical challenge to the status quo of the seventh-century-CE Arabian Peninsula. To challenge its polytheism was to be a threat to the sociopolitical order. No matter what the secularists say, every community has some sort of depiction of its god or gods, and when that depiction is challenged, it poses a threat to the society. Muhammad was concerned with social justice, for the poor and the weak, and by comparison to contemporary Arabian standards was more gracious to women than the polytheistic Arabian culture in which he found himself. Because of his monotheistic message, Muhammad was threatened, his early followers were persecuted in often grotesque ways—beaten, or tied down and exposed to the blazing Arabian sun—and the community was punished by economic and social embargoes for three years. This abusive treatment in Mecca was accompanied by Muhammad's teaching to his followers *not* to return like for like, *not* to retaliate or fight back.

But Muhammad's teaching changes: after the emigration to Medina, some two hundred miles away from Mecca, where Muhammad is invited to serve as a leader of the Medinan community, new direction is given. From this point forward it becomes legitimate to employ battle in pursuit of what the community believes to be justice. Some of the most important moments of early Islam recount significant battles in which it is believed that Muhammad is vindicated through military victory. When Muhammad returns some time later to Mecca, he does so accompanied by ten thousand troops, but the city receives him without a fight.

To summarize: the base founding narratives of the two traditions are different. Both are concerned with justice. Both seek the goal of peace. But Jesus advocates the way of nonretaliatory suffering love; he is killed; and his followers claim he is vindicated in his resurrection. Muhammad advocates the way of just employment of military might in service to justice; he employs this method and is victorious; and his followers claim he is vindicated by his victories. Both are concerned with the establishment of a just and peaceable order, but the two different traditions begin with two different *means* of the pursuit of this social order.

These are two very different stories. And they have profoundly different implications for those who live out of those stories.

One may find in Istanbul a magnificent display of artifacts of great historical import to the Islamic tradition, among them a sword of Muhammad, with which he brought an end to conflict between the warring Arabian tribes. But Jesus employed the way of the cross to deal with the conflict that afflicted humankind, was unjustly crucified at the hands of his enemies, and prayed for them while they killed him.

But—this is terribly important—the Christian tradition, as it were, uprooted the cross and used it as a sword. Even today in Arlington National Cemetery one finds that the cross no longer symbolizes a suffering love unto death, but rather symbolizes the dying that occurs while seeking to subdue or kill one's enemies in a cause thought justified. In other words, while the founding stories of Jesus's cross and Muhammad's sword are indeed profoundly different, the Christian tradition made the cross a tool of the sword, which brings us to the second main point.

2. The mainstream *of Christian tradition looks more like the Muhammad story than the Jesus story, and in some—alas, in many—cases, looks not nearly so noble. In fact, the mainstream of the Christian tradition has rejected the Jesus story as being relevant to the ethic of war and peacemaking and has employed other ethical systems for this purpose.*

Just as the teaching of Muhammad changed after the emigration from Mecca to Medina, so the teaching of the majority of the Christian tradition changed starting in the fourth century CE. Prior to that time, Christianity had been illegal and on occasion persecuted, in some cases severely. During this time, the early church fathers who addressed the question of whether it was legitimate for Christians to kill in war said on the whole that it was not. But this principled stance, of three centuries' duration, changed. By the end of the fourth century, pagan faiths were illegal, and Christianity the only legal faith in the Roman Empire. The persecuting power of empire became available to the church. And the alliances that developed between empire and church gave rise to a principled rejection of the Jesus-story logic in favor of a Muhammad-story logic. I do not mean, of course, that the church rejected the *name* of Jesus in favor of the *name* of Muhammad (who would not arise on the historical scene for several centuries), or that the church rejected a *claim* to the authority of Jesus in favor of a *claim* to the authority of Muhammad. I simply mean that the *formal shape*, the *basic logic*, of the church's understanding of the employment of force on behalf of justice was more like the subsequent teaching of Muhammad than the teaching of Jesus.

This is a terribly important development in the Christian tradition, as important as the change in Muhammad's stance when he emigrated from Mecca, where he first prescribed nonretaliation, to Medina, where he prescribed retaliation. But it must be noted that the nature of the shift in the Christian tradition is debated. It appears to most interpreters of Islam that the early "pacifism," if you will, of Muhammad was *strategic* as opposed to *principled*. That is, Muhammad counseled nonretaliation not as a matter of principle, not because he believed it to be the normal standard of what is good and right. Instead, he appears to have counseled nonretaliation in those early days in Mecca because it would have been a recipe for disaster had he done otherwise. The early movement would have been decimated and destroyed in short order by the Meccan elite. But once a power base was established in Medina, then the principle of retaliation, or the employment of military means in service to justice, was established. This strategic interpretation of the Meccan years is the only way one can make sense of the rest of the teachings of the Qur'an.

There are those who interpret the pacifism of the early church in the same way—as *strategic*. In this line of reasoning, the early church fathers counseled nonviolence because it would have made no strategic sense to serve the military might of an empire that was persecuting you. One would not feed with one hand the beast that bites and devours the other hand. While such an argument makes much sense, this is not—as we have seen—the primary thrust of the arguments made by the early church fathers. Moreover, the consistent message of the New Testament aligns with the *principled* teaching of the early church fathers: disciples of Jesus are commanded to employ suffering love in response to the sin of the world, not to take up the sword on behalf of justice.

And now two important subpoints. First, please note the deep irony of stereotypical American Christian critiques of Islam: *the Christian who points to the differences between Jesus and Muhammad is often the very same Christian who has rejected the Jesus story as relevant to the question of war.* The Christian may rightly claim that the Jesus story and the Muhammad story are different. But that same American Christian often then advocates war against Islamic militants; and he employs not the logic of Jesus but the logic of Muhammad, who taught that it is legitimate to make war against those we judge aggressors. Or, it should be more carefully said, to the degree that the American Christian argues for a restricted employment of force for the purpose of making peace, to that degree does he employ the logic of Muhammad; but to the degree that he employs all too often the logic of Rambo and crusading for "infinite justice" and "a war against terror," or that he will "drop the bomb on 'em all and let God sort it out," then his logic is not nearly so noble as that of Muhammad and indeed is barbaric in comparison.

Second, as we have seen, in many of the classical Islamic legal traditions, jihad (taken in the sense of battle) is in numerous ways more like the Christian Just War tradition that arises in the fourth century CE than it is like "holy war" or "total war." The particulars in some cases differ, but the formal structures parallel each other. And the particulars of the Christian JWT and the Islamic legal tradition in other cases are alike. For example, both are concerned that innocents, that is, nonmilitary personnel, not be killed in war.

But we American Christians have tended simply to equate jihad with "holy war." Many Muslims point out that one cannot find the phrase "holy war" anywhere in the Qur'an, and they find it offensive that "holy war" is so often used as a synonym for the Arabic word *jihad*. They know that war is never "holy" and that it must never be allowed to become the ruthless destruction of noncombatants.[1]

While this summarizes the major contentions of the book, there are three more important matters that I think are of great importance in the current conversations in American culture about the relations between Christianity and Islam, to which I now turn. First, that "religion" is not the problem. Typically in the "secular" West, it is thought that all our problems arise from "religions," which are particularly prone to violence. It is this contention to which I turn in chapters 15 and 16.

Second, I want to suggest that "Islamic culture" is not the problem. When the conflict between "Islam" and "the West" is discussed, polemicists often assert that Western culture and Islamic culture simply cannot coexist. Moreover, they contend, we are in the midst of a culture clash between two ways of life, and one will inevitably destroy the other. I suggest that the very definition of *culture* often employed by those who make such arguments is wrongheaded, and that stepping back from such arguments, we may find fascinating areas of overlap and shared concern between our different communities. I address this matter in chapters 17 and 18.

Finally, I want to return to a fundamental difference between Christianity and Islam, namely, the Qur'an's insistence that Jesus was not crucified. We must return to this very important difference between the two not as a lever for yet more animosity but as a ground for helping disciples of this crucified Jesus have yet more resources for being peaceable neighbors. I address this matter in chapter 19, followed by some closing observations in chapter 20.

15

Why "Religion" Is Not (Necessarily) the Problem

Visiting Abraham's Burial Place

One day I made my way to Hebron, the burial place of Abraham, Isaac, and Jacob. The trip is not advised by the US State Department, given that much of the West Bank is the locus of tension between Palestinians and Israelis. A large number of illegal Zionist settlers have taken up residence in Hebron; several sources report as many as four military personnel per settler, so the town looks like a war zone, with security forces and razor wire and checkpoints and observation towers scattered throughout the city center. Hebron has seen tragic incidents of violence and killing throughout the twentieth century, and the antagonism and hostility are palpable. I particularly wanted to visit representatives of Christian Peacemaker Teams, an organization committed to the practice of nonviolence, which purposefully enters situations of armed conflict to get in the way, to help keep violence at bay.

A kind American woman met me at the bus stop, nestled inside a noisy, bustling intersection of shops and pedestrians and vehicles. She ushered me further south, toward the region where the settlers have taken up their illegal residences. As we walked, she said she had someone she wanted me to meet—a longtime activist with the Palestinian Liberation Organization (PLO), a friend of Arafat's. He and I sat and had a soft drink together, enjoying one another's company, and he told tales of his life, the work he had done, and the prison sentences he had served, the physical signs of the torture he said he had received manifest on his body. We talked about peace and Palestine and Israel and the PLO and his family.

At one point I asked him about "religion." His response surprised me: leave religion out of it, he said. Oh yes, he went on, people get more religious when they get hungry and can't feed their children. But this is not about religion. It's about land and justice and people wanting to be able to make a living. I would be told this again and again by Palestinians—the struggle is not about religion. "Leave religion out of it; it only confuses the problem. The problem is *land*." I was also told this by a well-respected Palestinian Anglican priest; by the Muslim president of an Arab university in Palestine; by a nominally Christian administrator of a Palestinian university, who has been jailed numerous times, early on for his fighting with arms, and more recently for his fighting with Gandhian methods of nonviolent resistance; and by the spokesperson of the Nashville Muslim community.

Because of this unexpected experience, I am hesitant to make the claim I think needs to be made in this chapter, but I think it needs to be said anyway: the privatization of religion is not the solution we need. That is, to make religion private, leaving questions about justice and politics and society to the realm of the secular, will not do.

The Myth of Religious Violence

William Cavanaugh's book *The Myth of Religious Violence* teaches us this:[1] storytelling in the Western world typically assumes that it is possible to identify "religion" as some sort of thing separable from the "secular." Religion is construed as a universal human experience—of which things like Christianity, Islam, or Hinduism are species of the larger category. Moreover, because religion is typically

(a) absolutist, or (b) divisive, or (c) irrational, it is therefore more prone to violence than is the secular. The secular is thought to be the realm of peacemaking, not prone to such absolutism, divisiveness, or irrationality. The secular is pluralist and inclusive; religion is (more prone to be) violent and exclusivist. Cavanaugh cites Charles Kimball, who claims: "It is somewhat trite, but nevertheless sadly true, to say that more wars have been waged, more people killed, and these days more evil perpetrated in the name of religion than by any other institutional force in human history."[2]

Thus, the history of "the West" typically includes a tale in which a primary problem of Europe in the sixteenth and seventeenth centuries was the "wars of religion," in which Protestants and Catholics arrayed themselves to slaughter each other in the name of their particular religious traditions. The secular state arrives as a (secular) savior of sorts, to save European culture from the public relevance and public power of religion. Religion can be allowed to exist in the realm of the "private," but it can no longer be allowed a place in the public square.

For our purposes, note that a common critique of Islam runs this way: Christianity once mingled politics and religion (the Crusades are then trotted out as evidence) but moved beyond such medieval thinking. Christians know, these days, except for maybe a few backward fundamentalists, that religion and politics should not mix and that warring must never be done in service to religion. Muslims, on the other hand (so the critique continues), have not learned this lesson. They still want to mix religion and politics, religion and war. Islam is stuck in the Middle Ages and must modernize if we are going to make any progress. Religion must be *private*, and Muslims have, on the whole, failed as of yet to make that move.

So go such arguments. But Cavanaugh argues that when carefully examining this myth, one discovers that when scholars define religion—as something separable from politics or economics or the secular—the definitions ultimately fall in upon themselves. Though many assume it is a simple thing to separate the religious from the secular, it turns out not to be as simple as one might imagine. Instead, Cavanaugh argues that "religion" was invented by modernity. For the ancient and medieval Christians, there was no comparable notion of religion as employed in our language today. For us, religion

111

is something separable from the secular, a universal and timeless phenomenon of which Christianity and Islam and Judaism are particular instances.

But religion as a category separable from other components of life—such as politics, economics, culture—was simply not a given category in the ancient and medieval worlds. Thus, to make such an argument would be anachronistic. That is, to even argue such a claim would be nonsense. Cataloging the work of numerous scholars, Cavanaugh illustrates that religion is "an invention of the modern West."[3] But he wants to illustrate more: first, that the way in which religion gets defined "has a history, and what counts as a religion and what does not in any given context depends on different configurations of power and authority." And this then leads to a second, even more important, conclusion: that "the concept of religion that is separable from secular phenomena is *itself* part of a particular configuration of power," namely, the modern liberal nation-state. In the West, religion gets construed as a timeless, universal, interior, and private reality. Consequently, to call Christianity a religion is a way of separating "loyalty to God from one's public loyalty to the nation-state."[4] In other words, the way religion has been defined in the modern West is a power play—a power play to make it acceptable for Christians to think that their loyalty to God has no bearing upon their loyalty to the nation.

Consider one possible definition of religion, as an orientation toward that which is absolute. God is seen as absolute or transcendent in a way that the state or money or other cultural artifacts are not. Obviously, Jews and Christians and Muslims do indeed take God as absolute, beyond any other thing or person or community. But Jews and Christians (informed by the Ten Commandments) and Muslims (informed by the prohibition of making images) are well aware of the tendency to interpret one's understanding of the absolute in idolatrous fashion. Thus, for such believers the important question is *not* whether one makes a claim to believe in an absolute God but *what* or *which* god is actually being worshiped.

In other words, a definition of "absolute" is more helpful if it not only includes an intellectual proposition, such as "I believe in an absolute God," but also takes into account *behavior*. By examining behavior, we are better able to test the nature of the claim. To use Cavanaugh's example, one might claim to believe in God as the absolute but spend his Sundays on the sofa watching football and spend the rest of his week recklessly pursuing profits by playing the markets. Thus, one might actually be worshiping Mammon as opposed to the God revealed by Jesus. When Jesus spoke of Mammon in the Sermon on the Mount, he did not thereby mean that there is really a god called Mammon; he meant that the behavior of our lives makes absolute gods of things other than the true God.

Such testing of behavior, then, allows us to come full circle, to the question of violence. So, continues Cavanaugh, we should do such testing with some sort of "absolute" commitment, say, "that for which one is willing to kill."[5] To kill at the behest of another authority is obviously no small matter. It requires a substantive power indeed to command such an act. In this case, it becomes quite obvious that for American Christians, the nation-state has *more* "absolute authority" than the church—that the nation claims more absolute authority than anything we might call religion.

One might object that all this conversation is much ado about semantics: it is what you academics do, waste time defining words. But the point is much more important than a mere academic argument. My point, and one of Cavanaugh's points, is this: the "myth of religious violence" posits that the violence of religion is unacceptable, but the violence of the secular state is either ignored or seen as legitimate. The violence of religion is always necessarily irrational, but the violence of the state is seen as necessary for peacemaking. Once this assumption is swallowed, the violence of the state is justified, overlooked, ignored, or even celebrated by Western Christians, all while believing that the solution is for Islam to become more Western.

The myth—this is my summary, and not Cavanaugh's—has gutted the Christian faith and turned the pitiful, almost lifeless creature into a lapdog for the state. And meanwhile, the Christian celebrates how wonderful it is that the state allows freedom for the "Christian religion."

America as Savior

Nonetheless, there are enough fragments of the early Christian tradition in us, in spite of our tendency to "spiritualize," that we know history and culture matter. But given that Western liberalism has tended to compartmentalize "religion" into the realm of the private, what shall save the world? If religion is thought to be irrelevant to time and culture, then what will redeem human history? The answer: democracy and the American dream. The state can step, and has often stepped, into that space, putting itself forward as the savior of the world and its military might as the arm by which it saves.

Talal Asad, insisting that Western political liberal theory begins with the assumed right of self-defense (think of Hobbes, for example), notes this move and levels a devastating critique that the Christian community needs to hear: "The violence at the heart of liberal political doctrine makes this clear: the right to self-defense eventually calls for a project of universal redemption." What Asad means is not simply that Western democracies believe in the redemption of the world; he means that the nation-state usurps the role of Messiah and that the route to redemption is not through a cross but through wielding the sword on behalf of the intended universal redemption. America becomes the Messiah. "Another way of putting this is to say . . . that some humans have to be treated violently in order that humanity can be redeemed."[6]

Unfortunately, Asad sees the Christian doctrine of atonement as one expression of this belief. Asad does not spell this out, but I speculate that his thinking goes something like this: the Christian myth gets to "redemption" through a crucifixion, a violent, abusive act; "justice" demands such punishment; and redemption requires the shedding of blood in exchange for the sins and hostilities committed.

This myth—and I think "myth" is the correct description[7]—ironically depicts the cross in such fashion that it becomes easily co-opted by Crusaders of any and all sorts. As World War I historian Richard Gamble puts it, "Americans have been habitually drawn to language that is redemptive, apocalyptic, and expansive. Americans have long experienced and articulated a sense of urgency, of hanging on the precipice of great change. . . . They have fallen easily into the Manichean habit of dividing the world into darkness and light, Evil and Good, past and future, Satan and Christ. They have seen themselves as a progressive, redemptive force, waging war in the ranks of Christ's army, or have imagined themselves even as Christ Himself, liberating those in bondage and healing the afflicted."[8] The difference, of course, is that while Christ gave his life, these American Crusaders saw themselves as killing for Christ. Thus, there is a too often unstated distinction between the way of Christ and the way of the soldier, argues Gamble, who cites a politician giving a rallying cry at the time of World War I: "Christ gave his life upon the cross that mankind might gain the Kingdom of Heaven, while to-night we shall solemnly decree the sublimest sacrifice ever made by a nation for the salvation of humanity, the institution of world-wide liberty and freedom."[9]

Thus, yet again, another instance in which the cross is spiritualized, compartmentalized, its ethical significance and narrative logic ripped from it, and America-as-historical-Savior, which will hear nothing of carrying a cross, calls the disciples of that Jesus to leave their crosses and rid the world of war by war, not by the way of Christ.

A Parable

A king went out to conquer, amassing great wealth and power. There came to him a people who asserted that some other was king, whom they called "Lord of Lords." The king replied: you may freely worship this one you call "lord," you may freely build your buildings and write your books and seek your converts to this one you call "lord." But I shall rule the marketplace, and the army, and the public square. He shall be your personal "lord," while I am your public king. I shall make the laws, and you shall obey them. I shall tell you what enemies to kill, and you shall kill them. I shall give you a marketplace, and you shall seek to maximize your profits and keep all your profits, even at the expense of the poor, or the widow, or the stranger, and thence you shall pay taxes with which we shall wage war against all who threaten your freedom to worship your personal "lord."

And the people replied: We will gladly do as you say, O king. Indeed, we shall obey your laws. And we shall seek great profit and keep all for ourselves. And we will kill your enemies, for you, O king, have allowed us to pray to our personal lord in our houses of worship, in the privacy of our closets. Even more, O king, because you have allowed us to worship thus, we will denounce all those who do not exalt you, and we will proclaim that you have granted us the right to worship, and we shall profess that any who do not obey your laws or maximize profit or kill your enemies are no servants of the private Lord of Lords. We will hang your standard in our halls of worship, we will honor those who fight your wars, and we will celebrate those who heedlessly maximize profit. Oh, grant us such liberty as this, O king!

The king was pleased, and his new subjects served him well and were happy and satisfied.

16

The Oklahoma Bombing, and Why America Can Never Commit Terrorist Acts

Back in Oklahoma City

After visiting the Cowboy Museum, I made my first visit to the Oklahoma City National Memorial: the scene of the greatest domestic terror attack that ever occurred in US history. On April 19, 1995, Timothy McVeigh drove a rental truck packed with several tons of explosives directly in front of the north entrance to the Alfred P. Murrah Federal Building in Oklahoma City. On that pleasant spring morning, the truck exploded, shearing off the northern half of the building, killing 168 people, 19 of whom were children. The carnage was beyond comprehension. Now at the former site of the Murrah Building is a grassy lawn, protected by a low fence, the lawn bounded by pine trees, and on the lawn, a single chair for every victim of that horrid day, large chairs for the adults, smaller chairs for the children and babies. Now where that street once lay, along which the rental truck was driven, is a reflecting pool, bounded on east and west by great gates.

I was deeply moved and troubled and wept there in that place. But one item particularly caught my attention and surprised me. In the memorial museum, a small computer kiosk provides research on American domestic terrorism, and it reports that the idea for bombing the Murrah Building apparently first arose among a group in Arkansas, among a charismatic Christian commune called The Covenant, The Sword, and The Arm of the Lord (referred to as the CSA). Kerry Noble, one of the evangelists and pastors in the CSA, tells his story at length in *Tabernacle of Hate: Why They Bombed Oklahoma City*, a tale of an apparently sincere people who cared about Scripture, worship, and discipleship, who sold possessions and gave up social stability to establish a community they believed honored God. But co-opted by paranoia, and increasingly willing to employ violence in the name of righteousness, they formed the conviction that they were playing an important role in the inevitable war that would bring about the purification of America.[1]

One could read Noble's story this way: look, see, here is one more example of the violent religious fruitcakes of the world, one more example of the way in which religion is killing us. But even a very cursory reading of right-wing Christian militia materials indicates something often overlooked: what these groups are most often concerned with is *America*. That is, they are willing to fight and kill on behalf of what they believe *America* is supposed to be.

The Fight for America

So my point in this chapter is not to make an argument that McVeigh and his accomplice, Terry Nichols, were driven by their Christian faith to bomb the Murrah Building. In fact, it is not exactly clear who had contacts with whom and who knew what. But McVeigh and Nichols were deeply indoctrinated in the American militia movement and the far-right-wing ideology that supported it, and they were willing to kill mass numbers of people in service of what they believed to be necessary for "America." And it is also clear that McVeigh was trained by the US military and used those skills to execute the mass murder of the 168 victims in Oklahoma City.

McVeigh and Nichols also clearly had connections with circles that embraced a convoluted Christian faith that was mixed with racial hatred, fear of Communism, and a willingness to employ grave violence, all for the sake of a righteous "Christian" nation.[2] This broader cultural matrix included the prominent group the Posse Comitatus, which included such figures as "Reverend Gale." Gale was known for violent rhetoric; in a 1982 broadcast Gale proclaimed that the good white Christian citizens should take an official who violates the Constitution "to the most populated intersection of the township and at noon hang him by the neck [and then] take the body down at dark and that will be an example to those other officials who are supposed to be your servants that they are going to abide by the Constitution."[3]

Similar is the tragic story of Gordon Kahl, an American farmer caught up in his own hatred of the federal government. Kahl believed the government had denied its responsibility to honor the law and lordship of Jesus. "These enemies of Christ . . . threw our Constitution and our Christian Common Law (which is none other than the Laws of God as set forth in the Scriptures) into the garbage can." The "enemies" have "two objectives in their goal of ruling the world. Destroy Christianity and the white race." Thus, maintained Kahl, "we are engaged in a struggle to the death between the people of the Kingdom of God, and the Kingdom of Satan."[4] Kahl himself killed two federal agents in a shoot-out. He was later killed in another shoot-out, in which he shot a local law enforcement officer. He died when federal agents poured diesel fuel down a roof vent and set afire the house in which he was hiding out.

But how can one possibly sort out whether it was Gale's or Kahl's "religion"—as a thing separable from any other element of his thought or practice—that led to such violence? Kahl was not fighting for a way of life that required nonviolent love of enemies. He was fighting for a "Kingdom of God" that had to have a "Christian Common Law" and a nation-state as its embodiment. Reverend Gale was fighting for his interpretation of the US Constitution, which itself assumes the legitimacy of war-making in defense of that very Constitution. Kahl and Gale called for warfare because they thought the US Constitution—and the way of life it protected—to be threatened. And it must be noted that this is not merely a "conservative" phenomenon. No less than archliberal and Christian antagonist Christopher Hitchens makes a similar move when he argues that the preemptive war in Iraq was justified because it is what Western liberal values entail and require.[5]

Another illustration of this point is the recent and much discussed finding that evangelical Christians were one of the largest demographic groups generally supporting the legitimacy of torture. A recent Pew Forum survey on torture found a correlation between church attendance and the acceptance of torture. More than six in ten (62 percent) white evangelical Protestants found torture either "often justified" or "sometimes justified." It appeared that the more one attended church, and the more conservative one's Christian faith, the more one was inclined to accept the use of torture. But a follow-up article on the Pew site noted that "while the differences in opinion among religious groups are evident enough, the source of those differences is less clear." That is, party affiliation is more significant: "Differences between Republicans and Democrats are even larger than differences across religious groups, with 64% of Republicans saying torture can be often or sometimes justified, compared with only 36% among Democrats." These findings again raise the question: what is really at stake in our social policy commitments? Our religion? Or our understanding of the nature and role of America in the world today?[6]

Back to Kahl: angered by his death, others attempted in late 1983 to blow up a natural gas pipeline in Arkansas with dynamite, but only dented it. The leader of that attempt, Richard Wayne Snell, would rob pawnshops and give the proceeds to the CSA. Snell, also legitimating his crimes based upon his strained interpretation of Christian faith, believed that most owners of pawnshops were Jews and "deserved to die." So a week and a half following the failed pipeline incident, Snell robbed a pawnshop and murdered the owner, William Stumpp, who was not Jewish but an Episcopalian. In 1984, and in cold blood, Snell killed an African American state trooper, Louis Bryant. Some twelve years after the murder of Stumpp, Snell was executed on April 19, a date bearing significance in some right-wing circles. This was the day of the burning of the Branch Davidian compound at Waco, Texas. Twelve hours prior to Snell's execution, McVeigh bombed the Murrah Federal Building.[7]

Christian Church as Chaplain to America

On the outskirts of Oklahoma City, back at the Cowboy Museum, I had come across a life-sized model of a stereotypical nineteenth-century Western town. At one end of the exhibit's "Main Street" sat the "Christian Church." This is profoundly troubling. Hear Dee Brown again: all the "great myths of the American West"—"tales of fur traders, mountain men, steamboat pilots, goldseekers, gamblers, gunmen, cavalrymen, cowboys, harlots, missionaries, schoolmarms, and homesteaders"—arose out of the very same forces by which "the culture and civilization of the American Indian was destroyed."[8] And at the end of the mythical Cowboy Town on that mythical Main Street stands the Christian Church, chaplain to the imperial advance of "America."

Indeed, the church in America has typically stood by, sometimes silently but often in profuse praise of, the American project. Obviously, compared to other human governments, there are many things about the American project much preferable to other such projects. We can celebrate the manner in which the American project has evolved to include women and African-Americans as those counted as rights-bearing people.[9] We can celebrate the manner in which individual creativity and enterprise and ingenuity have been given space to flourish and prosper. We can celebrate the nonviolent transfer of power that happens with every election cycle. We can celebrate America's music and literature and food, its hills and rivers and mountains, its hardworking and generous and self-sacrificing people. There are many people who would be grateful to live in the midst of such blessings, and I am among them.

But to be grateful for such blessings cannot mean unqualified acceptance of the American agenda; it, like all nation-states and kingdoms and empires, is ultimately self-seeking. The American agenda, in the end, cannot submit itself to the fundamental politics of the Jesus story, in which the way of peace and righteousness advances through the way of cross and resurrection. Empires are not willing to suffer. Empires are not willing to die. Empires are not willing to practice nonviolent love of enemy. Empires, at their best, might aspire to the ethic of the Muhammad story: to employ war with restraint and as a last resort, and only in service to overthrow tyranny. But in practice, empires seldom attain such noble heights, and the American empire has been no exception to that rule.

Meanwhile, the Christian church in America has often sanctioned and blessed the terrorizing and violent ways of our empire. Indeed, the danger of telling Main Street Christians the sorts of tales I've told is the temptation simply to discount them: "We are more advanced than those early Puritans, and we would never treat a native population in such a manner. We are more educated than these far-right Arkansas woodsmen, and we would never be like the mass murderer Timothy McVeigh."

But the ease with which "we" seek to distance ourselves overlooks the apparently sincere and well-intentioned pursuit of Christian faith that undergirds such efforts. Consider the 102 instances of bombing and arson committed against abortion clinics from 1977 to 1987. During 1984 alone, thirty such incidents occurred. For example, James Simmons and Matthew Goldsby, described by friends and acquaintances as fine, well-liked "Christian young people," bombed three abortion clinics in Pensacola, Florida. Professors Dallas Blanchard and Terry Prewitt note that this Gideon Project, as the young people called it, was not "an irrational, deviant act committed by fanatics or psychopaths." Instead, their work, convictions, and deeds arose out of their seriously practiced charismatic and fundamentalist Christian faith. According to Kathy Simmons, her husband, Jimmy, received the notion of bombing "from the Lord, and He told him how to build it." After the bombing, Goldsby's girlfriend, Kaye Wiggins, called the bombings "a gift to Jesus on his birthday."[10] While Simmons and Goldsby took pains to kill no one, Rev. Paul Hill finally decided that his faith required that he kill abortion doctors. Whatever one makes of the numerous errors of biblical interpretation, one cannot escape that we have here a man who has taken his faith very seriously, and at least at the time of his writing in 2001 and 2003, held no regrets and firmly believed that the God of Jesus had led him to such action.[11]

Making Exceptions for US

But again, such behavior is easy for perhaps many if not most American Christians to discount as having any relevance to themselves. The extremism of fundamentalist Christians has been the (often unfair) laughingstock of mainstream American culture at least since the Scopes trial. But back in the National Memorial I found fascinating the definition of *terrorism* provided by the US government: "pre-meditated, politically motivated violence perpetrated against noncombatant targets by sub-national groups or clandestine agents, usually intended to influence an audience."[12]

He who defines the word wins the argument: a bit of conventional wisdom one learns in higher education. And the US government, in defining terrorism, thus exempts itself from any indictment for terrorism: by defining terrorism as "sub-national," the US could never, by definition, commit terrorism. And when we Main Street Christian church folks use "we"—"we are not like those backward fundamentalists"—do we not thereby exempt ourselves from any soul-searching for the ways in which we have supported and underwritten the much greater devastation of the imperialist projects of our government?

This was the question raised in an essay attributed to Timothy McVeigh prior to his execution by the state. McVeigh was a decorated US Army veteran of the first Iraq war, and he characterized US foreign policy as deeply hypocritical. The United States claims, says the essay, that "Iraq has no right to stockpile chemical or biological weapons ('weapons of mass destruction')." Yet, it continues, the US is precisely the country that set the precedent for the use of such weapons. We see the pictures of the Kurds killed by Saddam's chemical weapons, but why, the essay asks, are these pictures never set alongside pictures of women and children killed in Hiroshima and Nagasaki?[13]

Here, the mass murderer McVeigh raises important questions. The temptation, of course, is to be so disgusted with the horror of this man's own deeds that we assume we need not answer his questions, that merely to attend to the questions somehow justifies the questioner's wicked acts. But as noted previously, the critique of the apostle Paul assumes that we have all fallen under the same dynamic of evil; the task of judging necessarily entails that we judge ourselves. But we do not want to hear such words. We have at hand many easy justifications for our own horrors, our own burning of the paper cities of Japan in World War II; our dropping of the atom bomb;

our support of dictator Saddam Hussein; our napalming children in Vietnam; Sherman's marching and torching across the southern US; our taking up residence in Saudi Arabia; our massacres in the Philippines; and so forth. We are the good guys, and the good guys must do what is necessary to win.

This making exceptions for "us"—assuming that we are the good guys, and the enemy is not—has a long history, as Andrew Bacevich notes in his recent book *The Limits of Power: The End of American Exceptionalism.*[14] Bacevich is a conservative Catholic, a political conservative, a professor of history and international relations, and a retired army colonel. But his conservatism finds primary expression in distrust of human institutions wielding power. He thus distrusts "American exceptionalism," which claims that America has a special mandate by God to make things turn out right and is thus granted an exception to do the things others are not. American exceptionalism began, claims Bacevich, with the earliest arrival of Europeans on these shores and continues to this day, not merely unabated but increasingly militant, arrogant, and presumptuous, especially in the last forty years.

Thus we find not merely the dynamic of disciples of Jesus practicing terrorism but also what may be a more pernicious move, namely, imperialist power employing terror but insisting that it is not terror, indeed cannot by definition be terror, because we, after all, are the good guys.

17

On the Sign of Jonah,
and the "Clash of Civilizations" Thesis

The Sign of Jonah

One of the great ironies of the tale of Jonah is that the pagans in the story have more rightly formed piety than has the prophet. It is, after all, Nineveh—that great and ancient city of blood, situated in that cradle we now call Iraq—that repented, while the prophet did not. The tale of Jonah is a great and cautionary one: those whom one deems one's greatest enemies may be more open to the truth and the necessity of repentance than one's own professing people of God. It will not suffice merely to long for God to rain down fire upon one's enemies; the enemies may actually be closer to God than oneself. A troubling sign. Moreover, one's "enemies" may actually believe that we, the self-perceived righteous ones, are in fact that great Nineveh, that "city of blood." It is a possibility worth pondering at great length.

At a minimum, the moral of the Jonah tale teaches us again to seek first to understand, then to be understood; to practice "double vision"; to shut up and sit still long enough to listen to what the "Other" has to say. Indeed, there are many Muslims not only to whom Christians should pay attention but also from whom we will learn a great deal. One is scholar Talal Asad. In his book *On Suicide Bombing*, Asad insists—as a Western, Muslim academic—that he is *not* arguing that terrorism is ever justified. Instead, he wants to ask questions about Western liberalism in light of suicide bombing; that is, what can our reaction to suicide bombing tell us about ourselves? What does our distinction between terrorism on the one hand (always seen as illicit and immoral) and war-making on the other (not seen as immoral but even as a duty and honorable) tell us about ourselves? What is the important distinction for Western culture as to when killing is legitimate and when it is not? And along his route to answering some of those questions, Asad raises a particularly important question about the way in which the rhetoric of "culture" operates in America.

Back to that Independence Day when I lectured on some considerations for understanding Islam, Christianity, and war-making: a kind critic came to me afterward and stated in brief the notion that when East and West collide, one must give. Along the fronts of two cultures, they cannot peaceably coexist; one must yield to the other. One will be destroyed, the other ascendant. Similarly, another commentator put it this way: "Here's the bottom line. . . . The war today is between seventh-century Islamic culture and twenty-first-century modern culture. These cultures are incompatible. They cannot coexist because the values of one violate the values of the other."[1]

Asad engages at length this "clash of civilizations" thesis, which serves as a common schema for interpreting the contemporary wars between East and West. We saw previously that the thesis advocated by Western anthropologists runs as follows: Yes, Christians once perpetrated the Crusades, and parallel Islam's jihad. But Christianity has grown up, moved beyond such barbarism, while Islam has not. Militaristic jihad remains central to Islam. Thus, if there is to be peaceable coexistence, then Islam must put away its barbarism, as has Christianity. Otherwise, war is inevitable. "There is only one way to resolve the clash between seventh-century Islamic culture and the twenty-first century: Islamic culture has to change."[2]

We saw in previous chapters that after the problem with Islam is posed in this matter, the proposed solution is that Islam must "modernize" its notion of "religion" by privatizing it. Moreover, we saw how this move only makes the adherents of a faith tradition more susceptible to being co-opted by the nation-state. We have also seen earlier that both Christian faith and Islamic faith are always and necessarily political—that is, our relationship with God cannot be separate from our relationship with our neighbors.

But Asad asks a different question in response to the "clash of civilizations" thesis. He asks whether "culture" can ever be understood as a single *thing* that can be rejected, withdrawn from, or accepted as a whole. Moreover—against the many ill-formed arguments of Christians who argue that Islam is a culture, while Christianity is not—the gospel cannot be separated from culture. If *culture* simply denotes a given community's patterns of living together—how they eat together, how they deal with offenses, how they treat enemies, how they orient their lives toward their Creator, how they treat wealth, how and whether they give gifts, and so forth—then Christianity undeniably has specific cultural practices, which will take a variety of shapes in different settings and locations and contexts. *Culture* simply denotes an amalgam of various practices, commitments, and values.

Selective Discernment

With regard to particular contexts and places, Christianity has always had to practice "discerning and selective engagement," as Rodney Clapp puts it.[3] Christianity has always rejected prostitution, has sometimes accepted war and the charging of interest on loans, and has always practiced the eating of bread and the gathering together regularly for worship. One can neither accept nor reject *in whole* any culture. We are always selectively engaging, rejecting, accepting, and transforming.[4]

Thus, it is unhelpful and false to say that we have a "clash of civilizations," as if one can simply separate East and West, "Islamic culture" and "Christian culture." Undoubtedly, architecture and language and foods characterize East and West. The burka might characterize one, perhaps the bikini the other; Arabic the seemingly official language of one, English these days of the other. Minarets might characterize Islam, steeples Christianity. But then again, cultures are complex and multifaceted, comprising many different sorts of commitments, practices, and values. "Southern culture" —as I always liked to say to some of my midwestern colleagues in graduate school, when they got to looking down their nose at things southern—actually means all the things that make America interesting, like rock, country, and jazz music; Flannery O'Connor and Ernest Hemingway; barbeque and fried chicken. Southern culture also comprises certain social skills, such as speaking to complete strangers encountered on the sidewalk, or learning to say "ma'am" and "sir" as a sign of respect for one's elders. "The South" also means NASCAR (I did, after all, grow up in Talladega) and dirt-track car racing, beautiful Gulf Coast beaches and the tail end of the Appalachians, Bible Belt civil religion and consistently low-ranking public school systems, the KKK and a racism that is at once strangely polite and simultaneously ruthless in its so-called conservatism, longleaf pines and red clay soil, deep blue autumn skies and small-town Friday-night football games.

But even my very brief description is itself an *interpretation* of "the South." Any description of culture is selective. Southern blacks give different descriptions of the South than do southern whites. Moreover, southern blacks who are under the age of twenty-five give a different interpretation than do blacks who are over sixty. College-educated good ol' boys give different descriptions than do Yankee preppies. Hollywood, in all its self-righteous glory, inevitably portrays southern culture in a manner that any self-respecting southerner finds utterly and ironically intolerant. Daisy Duke and Boss Hogg do not the South make. I prefer Atticus Finch, myself, without any delusion that we do not have plenty of southern shortcomings.

Moreover, no culture ever stands still. Cultures constantly evolve, simply because cultures never arise out of a vacuum. Those who are fearful of losing particular traits of southern culture—I am sometimes among them—must remember that even those things we treasure were themselves gifted to us from other times and places. Rock and jazz and the blues would not be what they are apart from the contributions of the African slaves who were kidnapped and brought to these shores across the Middle Passage, who sang to us, as W. E. B. Du Bois put it, their "sorrow songs." Flannery O'Connor could not have been what she was without the inanities of Bible Belt fundamentalism. And Bible

Belt fundamentalism could never have become what it is apart from nineteenth-century German biblical scholarship.

Which is all to say that there is no *single* "Christian culture." There are certain practices that are specifiably Christian, but not a whole culture that is Christian as such. The Christian community always has to pick and choose. Moreover, there is a great diversity of judgment among Christians themselves about appropriate cultural expression of one's faith. Just as the burka is absolutely required in some Muslim contexts, ignored in others, and hotly debated in still others, so goes the bikini in various Christian contexts. "Mixed bathing," going to the prom, and wearing shorts in public are, to some southern Christian communities, high on the taboo list, while other Christian communities look with disdain upon any church community that even questions such things. Whether of Western culture, Bible Belt culture, or southern culture, Christian communities always make discerning judgments about what can be embraced, what can be rejected, and what we might seek to transform or convert or redeem. Some Christians have moved away from chicken and pork, given industrialized cruelty to animals; and Muslims and Jews will generally not eat pork barbecue, because their specific teachings do not allow the eating of pork. But I have eaten some very fine meals with Muslims that I have enjoyed every bit as much as the fried chicken I invariably ate with the parishioners of Locust Grove Church of Christ in rural Kentucky as a preacher during my college years. When I go to a Muslim's house, I prepare to remove my shoes, but I don't prepare to eat pork barbeque. And my "Christian culture" can do so with great and deep enjoyment and gratitude.

Shared Cultural Practices

Thus, when "encountering Islam," Christianity does not have to reject "Muslim culture," even "seventh-century Muslim culture," as a whole. Indeed, as I've tried to indicate, such a move would simply not even be possible and is intellectually convoluted. Certain elements of Islamic culture should be celebrated among Christians. I must confess that after spending time with one particular Muslim scholar in Jerusalem, I returned home chastened regarding not spending more time with my parents. (We were to meet at eight o'clock in the morning on the Saturday prior to my departure, and he arrived late, apologized, and said that he knew if he did not stop by his parents' prior to our meeting, he would "not see them today." "You see them every day?" "Yes, most every day.") Similarly, Muslim families in America will struggle with many of the same questions as do Christian families in America: how can we raise children not addicted to technology, illicit sexuality, or other substances? How can we raise children with the virtues of contentment, modesty, and compassion, in a culture that celebrates greed, exhibitionism, and steely-eyed ambition? How can we teach our children to pray, read, and discern well? How can we teach our children to honor the poor, needy, and marginalized, especially in the face of the billions of dollars arrayed to capture their wills in service to Mammon? These are all questions and concerns to which Christian and Muslim neighbors must both attend—and moreover, to which we can help each other attend. Muslims are quite right to remind us Christians that Western capitalism has indeed corroded families and the "traditional values" that we deem important. It may very well turn out that Muslims might be able to help us as much as—or more than?—James Dobson does in learning how to raise cohesive families in the face of Western liberalism, because they sometimes see the deeper failings of Western liberalism better than even the conservative Christians, who are often, in fact, deeply committed to the Western too-often-unthinking celebration of individualism and "free markets," which have created many of the difficulties we now face.

There will be other elements of the Muslim tradition and Qur'anic teaching that Christians will, of necessity, have to reject: such as the Qur'anic teaching that Jesus was not crucified; the permission given to retaliatory war-making; the claim that Muhammad most faithfully reveals to us the will of God. Such rejections are, of course, profoundly important elements of our faith. And serious Muslims, I suspect, will undoubtedly reject our rejection of these things. But it does not change the point being made here: culture cannot be engaged as a whole but only in varying parts. We must make selective judgments. There is no culture that can be rejected *in whole*.[5]

If a "culture" cannot be rejected as a whole, then why the widespread popularity of the "clash of civilizations" thesis? Asad says that it is seldom noted, especially among Western historians, that "for many centuries after the early conquests the majority of the populations in countries with Muslim rulers remained Christian, active as such in many spheres of public life."[6] We need not romanticize this contention—clearly, Christians under Muslim rulers often had second-class citizenship, just as Muslims and Jews had second-class citizenship under Christian imperial authorities. It does, however, challenge the "clash of civilizations" thesis.

So, whence the "clash of civilizations" thesis? Asad continues: "It was only with the Crusades that the papacy promoted the ideology of a unified Christendom at war with a unified Islam."[7] This is a deeply ironic observation. If it is true, then the "clash of civilizations" thesis—in which Western Christians claim that they have moved beyond Crusades thinking, while Muslims have not—is premised upon Crusader logic itself. Perhaps we are more like the Crusaders than we would have ever dreamed.

18

On Muslim Hospitality

I suggested earlier that cultures can be neither rejected nor accepted as a whole, and that instead given cultures will have some practices we celebrate, some we will want to modify or transform, and some we will need to reject altogether. I tend to think that Southern hospitality is an example of an American cultural practice that Christians, Jews, and Muslims can all celebrate: the guest received with honor, regardless of social status or position or wealth. It has been my privilege to sit at tables set by other hosts at which the homeless and the blind and the poor and the wealthy and the glamorous and the homely have all been welcomed. My parents and my in-laws and my wife and my extended family and my church family and my university family have all exhibited this good practice, and I have learned much watching them. It is part of the ancient wisdom, going back to Abraham, the patriarch of Jews, Christians, and Muslims alike, that one may entertain angels unawares; it is part of the ancient story of Jesus, especially as told by the Gospel of Luke, that the table embodies a special place of grace, in which the reconciliation offered by God to the world may be made manifest. The table is a sacred place, where one may encounter all sorts of mysteries, may encounter manifestations of reconciliation unexpected and surprising. And I also suspect that the political shape of Christian discipleship will have a much more profound impact upon the world by taking the table seriously than will any sort of quest for dominating power.

A similar sort of tradition around the table exists in Islam. Snjezana Akpinar notes that

> for Muslims, the concept of hospitality goes deeper into history than is commonly understood in the West. It is a virtue that lies at the very basis of the Islamic ethical system. For Arabs in particular, hospitality is an ancient concept. Pre-Islamic Arab civilization saw hospitality as a humanizing element that involves both the guest and host, creates trust between them, leads to an ennobling and transformative moment, and evokes a restorative energy crucial for the survival of the human race. Linked closely with honor and chivalry, hospitality was considered an act of unconditional surrender to the needs of others. Islam accepted this heritage at its very inception.[1]

Until a year ago, I had never eaten or taken tea or drunk coffee with Muslims, either as host or guest. Since then, it has been a grand adventure: drinking a Coca-Cola with a twenty-year member of the PLO, a colleague of Arafat, at a tiny shop in Hebron; breaking the Ramadan fast at the mosque here on Twelfth Avenue in Nashville, the same mosque about which I had been told that all the Muslims there wanted to "kill us"; taking tea with Professor Sari Nusseibeh, activist, author of a beautiful memoir on his life in Palestine, and president of Al Quds University in East Jerusalem; eating breakfast in Istanbul, complete with cream and honey, with a writer and a university administrator; eating pizza with the spokesperson for the Nashville Islamic community, a highly trained specialist and medical doctor at one of the world's leading research institutions—immediately following which I received an email from him showing that some vandals had that very morning defaced a local mosque, spray-painting Crusader crosses, along with an inscription telling the local Muslims to "go home."

My first meal as a guest in a Muslim home was fabulous. I found myself along with an esteemed professor and priest, Fr. David Burrell—whom I had known in passing as a graduate student at the University of Notre Dame—trekking through the streets of East Jerusalem, a stone's throw from the Garden of Gethsemane. We made our way to the home of an equally esteemed Muslim professor of theology, Professor Mustafa Abu Sway, a theologian at Al Quds University, the Arab-Palestinian university in East Jerusalem. Welcomed warmly by the family, we removed our shoes (yet another southern tradition I rather appreciate) and sat in the living room, where we enjoyed a spectacular view of the Dome of the Rock, just across the valley below us. We enjoyed, too, a fantastic meal, wonderful conversation, and numerous kind gestures of hospitality.

I would have several opportunities to meet with Mustafa during my stay in Jerusalem: he would patiently tutor me on some basic considerations and issues of Islam, would suggest questions I had not yet considered, would show me ways to transliterate important Arab words. We would spend some hours together later at the American Colony Hotel, later again at Tantur Ecumenical Institute. While his knowledge of Islam and responses to the particular research questions I raised were immensely helpful, perhaps more important was what often happens when one eats with another: I encountered him as a kind and caring human being, struggling with the realities of existence in occupied Palestinian territory. His children were respectful and gracious, his wife welcoming and well attired. She had cooked all day for us; meanwhile, Mustafa had done the dishes. ("I am no good at cooking," he said with a smile.) I came to understand that though we were very different and had different ultimate claims upon our lives—he the Qur'an and the teaching of Muhammad, I the lordship of Jesus and the calling to Christian discipleship—we still could and did share all sorts of important commonalities.

I would come to realize, for example, that his academic work entailed critiques both of the West and of the Islamic tradition that paralleled the sort of anti-imperialist critiques I had been trying to make in my own academic work. We were both trying to sort out what it meant to take seriously one's faith in the midst of competing powers. Mustafa had written his dissertation on Al Ghazali, the medieval professor par excellence in the Islamic world who, unlike the too-commonly-heard stereotypes of Muslims as self-serving and concerned only with acquiring an indulgent eternity in the afterlife, realized upon introspection that he performed his work and faith not simply for the sake of the love of God. So he gave up fame and wealth, and lived an unknown life for eleven years.[2]

I would quickly come to realize as well that Palestinians face hardships we Americans would find intolerable. For instance, Mustafa and his family had spent nearly $70,000 over three years' time in an attempt to acquire a building permit to build a new home, while a block away another illegal Israeli-settlement high-rise was going up. I came to appreciate that he would say what, as noted earlier, I heard other Palestinians, both Christians and Muslims, say: that the conflict in Palestine is not about religion, but about land and sustaining a living and justice and the dehumanizing effects of the existing "security" policies. I came to appreciate his concerns about raising families; he said in a lecture I heard him deliver, when asked what he worries about regarding raising a family in Palestine: "I worry about my children being exposed to radical political movements, too much materialism, the electronic jungle too many are surrounded with." And I knew that I was concerned with the very same questions in raising a family in the buckle of the Bible Belt; and I knew that my own Western culture was, on the whole, contributing more to the problem than to the solution.

The media can so narrow our fears upon "the enemy" that we fail to see common enemies we may face along with our Muslim neighbor: threats to family life, to sober life, to quiet and sensible work. The enemy identified centuries ago by St. Hilary of Poitiers is the same that many Muslims face and see with greater clarity than Westerners so deeply shaped by consumerist impulses: "We are fighting today against a wily persecutor, an insinuating enemy, against Constantius the antichrist, who does not scourge the back, but tickles the belly, who does not condemn to life but enriches to death, who instead of thrusting men into the liberty of prison, honours them in the slavery of the palace . . . who does not cut off the head with the sword, but slays the soul with gold."[3]

This was not to say that Mustafa had no cautionary or critical words for the West. When one audience member asked, "Do you have any fear of nuclear annihilation from Iran?" he promptly responded, "Never. We know the country that has used it: neither Sunni, nor Shiite, and it's not Iran." All we Americans knew the country that had used it too. Indeed, he knew the issue was very often about profits and power: "Nuclear proliferation is lucrative, and allows defiance." Just as many Western Christians grapple with such questions, so did he: he described the immense expenditures on nuclear arsenals as "absolutely harmful." It was "immoral," he said, that Arabs accounted for the purchase of such a large percentage of the weapons purchased from 1980 to 1990. He described this social strategy as "bunk." There is plenty of wealth, but it is wasted on extravagant city projects and weapons, instead of spent building universities and cultivating spirit. Technology, which should be employed in useful fashion, is instead often wasted on extravagance and "is an addiction sometimes." We spend exorbitant amounts on sending space probes to Mars; perhaps we should first put our own planet in order, raising questions about the shameful discrepancies of wealth between Northern and Southern Hemispheres.

The question of consumerism was, he said, "a difference of loss of way of life," and it brings about a strange sort of prioritization. Thus, he recounted that while traveling in a rural, impoverished area of South Africa, he came upon a Kentucky Fried Chicken; upon leaving the mosque in Mecca on *hajj*, he found a Starbucks. "A hamburger is a hamburger," he would go on to say, "but the question is one of deforestation." The Qur'an teaches, on the one hand, not to be cheap, and on the other, not to be extravagant. Muhammad taught that men ought not to wear gold or silk (but permitted it for women) and that women's dresses should not have trains. That is, wealth should serve you, not overwhelm you; do not busy yourself with it, accumulating it, for the pursuit becomes a wall between yourself and the spiritual life. Echoes of *Walden*? "Yes," he admitted, "I love it. And I love the place. I went there."

Regarding warfare, there are of course Islamic militants. "They are militant because of their context, and they don't flip [read] the Qur'an." And those who do, he added, don't really have access to it in Arabic. "The invasion of Iraq is a shame. All the pretexts were shown to be false." Saddam was a dictator, yes, but there are others. And if a country decides to deal with a dictator, they should operate within the sanctions and auspices of the UN. The militants are such because of colonial and neocolonial projects, he said, and some of them defy the Islamic code of ethics. The earliest Muslims, he noted—and as we have already seen—were strict pacifists, but then war came to be treated as a last resort; and if it comes, there are strict limits. Today these conditions are impossible to keep in war. Thus, we must not go to war. And in order not to go to war, we need to know each other. And knowing each other—as in marriage—entails difficult issues that must be dealt with and worked through. We Muslims and Christians, he continued, will continue to have substantive theological differences, as do Catholics and Protestants, but essentially we must respect each other as different but having a shared humanity.

"In one case," he said, "my mother breast-fed the baby of her Christian neighbor" who was unable to do so herself. Mustafa's mother "understood Islamic jurisprudence," so that he and his siblings "became brothers and sisters" with the Christian child and thus "could not marry."

Farther north in East Jerusalem, I made my way one day to the office of Professor Sari Nusseibeh. The president of Al Quds University, an activist for peace and a well-respected academic, Nusseibeh is well known in Israel and Palestine. He graciously made time for tea and conversation in the midst of a hectic schedule. I was met first by his security detail and then ushered in after a brief wait. Nusseibeh's beautiful memoir, *Once upon a Country: A Palestinian Life*,[4] provides a Palestinian perspective on the current impasse and hostility. But what I found most striking, both about his book and about Nusseibeh himself, was his graciousness in the midst of a situation in which he and his family had faced so many difficulties and intense persecution. Nusseibeh would be struck early in life with the importance of "double vision," though he never uses that term. He grew up in the city of Jerusalem, after the 1948 War, where a no-man's-land divided Jews from Arabs. He would gaze across the no-man's-land at bearded men wearing black clothing and wide-brimmed hats and wonder who they were, these Others across the chasm. Reading Jewish author Amos Oz's account of Oz's own childhood—imagining military strategies for defending the Jews from perpetrators of new crimes against his people—Nusseibeh realized Oz had no good stories of Arabs in his childhood. And then Nusseibeh wondered about his own childhood: "What had my parents known of [the Jews'] world? Did they know about the death camps? Weren't both sides to the conflict totally immersed in their own tragedies, each one oblivious to, or even antagonistic toward, the narrative of the other? Isn't this inability to imagine the lives of the 'other' at the heart of the Israeli–Palestinian conflict?"[5]

Nusseibeh's family story is one of loss: of property, community, and health. His father, a prominent figure, lost his leg in the fighting of the War of 1948. His mother's family lost their estate, and she would speak for years of the rolling hills covered with groves of fruit trees that extended down toward the Mediterranean Sea. His mother habitually struggled with resentment toward the Zionists "who plotted to take over her country, who'd shot her husband's leg off, and whom she held responsible for her father's early death, the uprooting of her ancient roots on the coastal plain, the despoiling of her homeland, and the exile of her mother. Even her dear father's grave was now in inaccessible enemy territory."[6]

For Nusseibeh, "religion" was meant to be a unifying rather than an estranging force: quoting from his father's manuscript describing the days around the War of 1948, "Religion, being essentially universal and one, should be made to serve the end of uniting the world rather than separating it." His mother's version of Islam "inculcated in us . . . a religion with minimal miracles—Mohammed's nocturnal ride on his magical steed is one of the few I can think of—and a cornucopia of rock-solid humanistic values. For her, Islam taught dignity, honesty, self-worth, simplicity, kindness, and of course love. Endless love. It was also flexible enough to change with the times. . . . In her Islam, there was also no competition among faiths."[7] In contrast, "the only place to meet the sort of wild-eyed fanatics who pose as Islam's spokesmen today would have been in old musty stories of Sheikh Qassam, or in St. George's library collection of Victorian-era horror novels."[8]

Nusseibeh sought opportunity to understand the Other, as, when a young man, he sought to stay at a kibbutz, which was an agricultural settlement, an experiment in socialist living. From the perspective of the Palestinians, the kibbutzniks "were the shock troops of the Israeli system, merciless Spartan soldier-farmers on the front line of every fight. I wanted to see for myself where the swords of Zion were being fashioned."[9] And he reports that he found fascinating, "high-caliber" people in the "enemy territory." They were idealistic, well-meaning people, with high humanist values, who simply gave little consideration to the fact that the land on which they were living, and the freedom they were enjoying, had been extracted at a high price from the Arab Palestinians, who never crossed their minds. From 1948 to 1967, the Arab Palestinians were "out of sight, out of mind." And the fact that they thought little of this cost to the Arabs was, he discovered, not due to ill will or malevolence. It was simply that "their humanism never had to face us."[10] It is—it occurred to me—the same as our good Christian living in the Bible Belt: we too celebrate our freedoms and way of life, and it never crosses our minds that such enjoyment was extracted at such a high price from those who lived on the land prior to us.

So on a number of occasions Nusseibeh says that he simply did not know what to do with such situations. What should be done? Who was to blame? "They were without question fine people, despite their blind spots. Didn't we have our own? I concluded from all this that ignorance, rather than some undefined evil intent, had to be at the core of our conflict."[11] He recounts that part of the wisdom he lives by, taken from the Muslim philosopher about whom he wrote his dissertation, is "quietly doing your best to humanize an 'imperfect society.'"[12] Engaging both Christian and Muslim activists as a university teacher, he and his wife, Lucy, would join Palestinian Christian Mubarak Awad, "a crusader for nonviolence and a proponent of Gandhi's civil disobedience." Lucy later joined Awad to start the Palestinian Center for the Study of Non-Violence, in Jerusalem.[13]

Near the end of our conversation, realizing the toll his work and convictions had cost him, I asked him one last question: "What has kept you going?"

"Islam," he said, "that is, 'submission to God.'"

I went away humbled and grateful for having had the opportunity to visit with him. He asked his bodyguard to drive me back into the city. On the return trip, the bodyguard told stories of the dangers Nusseibeh has faced. He clearly cared very much for his boss and obviously and dearly loved his own wife and children. I exited the SUV, stepping into the bustle and noise of East Jerusalem, wishing more knew of the compassion and humility and self-sacrificing service of the good Muslims I was meeting, and would continue to meet.

19

Good Friday

> The cross is not a detour or a hurdle on the way to the kingdom, nor
> is it even the way to the kingdom; it is the kingdom come.
>
> —John Howard Yoder, *The Politics of Jesus*

Taking Stock

I have suggested that the mainstream of Christian tradition, with
its Just War tradition, looks more like the Muhammad story than
the Jesus story. And more: that too often, the Christian has not
taken the constraints of the JWT seriously, so that war and exces-
sive brutality are increasingly justified. In the last four chapters, I
have suggested that the privatization of religion is no solution to the
perceived conflict between Christianity and Islam—for this move
has only given the nation-state an idolatrous power to use its war-
making powers in unaccounted-for imperial pursuits. The perceived
conflict between East and West, moreover, cannot be reduced to a
conflict between two different cultures, because cultures are mixed
and varied, an amalgam of lots of things. Moreover, there are many
cultural practices of Muslims that Christians can and should enjoy
and celebrate—such as hospitality, in which we welcome one another.

And in the giving and receiving of hospitality, we may discover all sorts of other fascinating things about each other.

To conclude, I want to focus again upon a fundamental difference between Christianity and Islam. I do so because I think that this particular difference will give us the ground to be better neighbors.

The Qur'an's Rejection of a Crucified Jesus

The Qur'an clearly holds Jesus in high esteem. But the monotheism proclaimed by Muhammad could not make sense of a Trinity that was not somehow detrimental to the oneness of God, and thus Jesus is not the Second Person of the Trinity but a faithful prophet of God. Moreover, according to the Qur'an, Jesus was not crucified. The Qur'an reports that some say, "We slew the Messiah Jesus son of Mary, Allah's messenger," but goes on to assert, "They slew him not nor crucified, but it appeared so unto them; and lo! Those who disagree concerning it are in doubt thereof; they have no knowledge thereof save pursuit of a conjecture; they slew him not for certain, But Allah took him up unto Himself. Allah was ever Mighty, Wise" (4:157–58).

Such an assertion, of course, threatens to do away with the historic event that Christians proclaim to be the very basis of their salvation. But the *way* in which we perceive it to be the basis of our salvation may have a profound impact upon our understanding of war and violence. For many American Christians, for example, the crucifixion is reckoned as an event propitiating the anger of God. The cross is the place of God's punishment upon the One who substitutes his life for the sin of humankind. God's anger thus expended, we may receive forgiveness of sins. We may be saved and go to heaven when we die. If this is the primary lens through which the crucifixion is understood, then the Qur'anic assertion that Jesus did not in fact die in crucifixion seems to undercut the very basis of heavenly salvation, removes the very possibility of atonement and reconciliation.[1] This view is called "penal substitutionary atonement." Jesus's death is understood as a substitute punishment for the punishment humankind deserved. Many Christians in the West see this as the only lens through which the meaning of Jesus's cross can be understood. Ironically, so do many Muslims.

But it is a historical fact that this interpretation is a relatively recent arrival on the scene of the history of Christian doctrine.[2] Numerous works in the last three decades have documented that the early church understood the cross in different terms: it was the triumph of suffering love over the powers of death and sin personified in Satan.[3] The principalities and powers—historically manifested in the imperialist and nationalist authorities that connived and conspired to kill Jesus—always overreach, and arrogantly vaunted themselves against the Son of God. And they were undone through suffering love. As the letter to the Colossians puts it, the *crucifixion* was the place of *victory* over the powers. In the crucifixion, Jesus "disarmed the rulers and authorities and made a public example of them, triumphing over them" (2:15).

As I put my ten-year-old to bed the night of Palm Sunday, he asked, "Why do they call Good Friday 'Good Friday,' when it was the day they killed Jesus?" One way to answer that insightful question is with the words of John Yoder: "The cross is not a detour or a hurdle on the way to the kingdom, nor is it even the way to the kingdom; it is the kingdom come."[4] That is, if the kingdom is present where God's will is done on earth as it is in heaven, then that is precisely what we witness in the way of the cross in the face of the unjust and domineering powers: the cross as place of obedience, which trusts that God will overcome the powers of oppression through suffering love, instead of retaliatory violence. The powers always assume that they can cow us into obedience through wielding the big stick of violence and death: do what we tell you, or we will defame you, or imprison you, or torture you, or kill you. So Pilate says to Jesus: "Do you not know that I have power to release you, and power to crucify you?" (John 19:10).

But Jesus, it appears, had set out upon a very different sort of saving mission. Muhammad would seek to save the Arabian tribes through a measured, just employment of military might, just as Christians would seek to do starting in the fourth century, and just as American Christians often seek to do in the twenty-first century. Indeed, many of Jesus's contemporaries expected Jesus to do precisely that: to take up the sword and deal with the Romans, to respond to the historical sin that kept Israel suffering under the malaise of imperial oppression. But Jesus chose a different way. At the start of Jesus's ministry, the tempter said, "If you are the Son of God," if you are really the one designated to bring about the work of God in the world, then just feed the masses, reform the temple, or become an emperor. The means and methods lay at hand for Jesus to make things turn out right, to use the mechanisms of coercive power politics to bring forth the kingdom of God. But after his forty days in the wilderness, Jesus set out as a Messiah who forsook taking up the sword to defend himself or—more troubling—to defend his beloved neighbor.

Even as he hung upon the cross, there would be those who would mock him, spit upon him, castigate him, because he did not fulfill their particular messianic expectations: "If you are the Son of God, come down from that cross." Crucifixion is no way for the work of God to be done in the world. What is desired is defeat of enemies, subjugation of enemies, destruction of enemies.

Theodicy

In seminary, when I was first beginning to seriously grapple with the question of Christians and war-making, I came upon yet another theological assertion I had never considered: that the cross of Jesus is a theodicy. A *theodicy* is an attempt to explain the ways of God. More specifically, how does one explain the reality of evil in the world? How does one explain the suffering of innocents? How does one explain unjust suffering if God is indeed all good and all powerful? Because I had always considered Jesus's crucifixion merely as a propitiation of God's anger, a sacrifice that had to be made so I could go to heaven, I could not possibly see how the cross of Jesus could even be construed as a theodicy.[5]

But I should be more careful here. A theodicy is typically understood as giving an *answer* to the questions, why is there evil in the world? and, why is there unjust suffering? But the crucifixion and Holy Week do not give us an *answer* to these questions. They do, however, provide a *response* to these questions, namely this: God enters into our suffering, suffers with us, suffers because of us, suffers in place of us. In Jesus, God absorbs the injustice, takes it on, wages battle with it through suffering love instead of the sword, or coercive power, or amassing of wealth, or by making history turn out right. Jesus is not waging battle merely with an abstraction. Jesus is not seeking to defeat the abstraction we call "sin" but the very real and historical powers of alienation and hostility and hatred and animosity and lust and greed and oppression, whether made manifest in very personal or in very institutionalized terms. Indeed, all battles in human history arise from such lust and pride and ego, both personalized and institutionalized. Sometimes oppression seems to take willful shape, as in the expression of dictators and presidents and tyrants; sometimes violence is mundane and apparently lacks personal will; sometimes it seems reducible to the tragedy of a "fallen" nature, whatever that means. Yet, whatever its manifestation, it is real. It kills, steals, destroys; makes lamentation, grief, tears.

It is Maundy Thursday as I write this. As we gathered to remember the stations of the cross last night, we remembered the brokenness of the world. I found myself overcome with grief, for the stations reminded me: *we killed you*, O Jesus. We were so threatened by the truth that you spoke, that we killed you, for you threatened to undo the social order, to unravel the status quo, and we were fearful of the manner in which you sought to save us.

Evil as Mundane

During my brief sojourn in Israel and Palestine, I would trek back up the hill every evening to the beautiful study institute in time for dinner. On two of those occasions, making my way up the hill after long days, I found myself cursing mad. "God damn it all to hell," I kept saying over and over again, angry with the senseless brutality: people dying at checkpoints because they did not bring along their papers and thus were not allowed to go to the hospital; young men arrested in the night and held without charges; a young boy, a resident of a refugee camp who had thrown stones at soldiers and was shot through the belly by a high-powered rifle; a young woman, visiting her father, in a café just outside Jerusalem, killed when a suicide bomber came upon the scene; the horror testified to at Yad Vashem, the Holocaust museum in Jerusalem. The apparently intractable, senseless, and fearful violence that characterizes human existence had overwhelmed me.

It is not something that can be simply reduced to human willfulness either. It is this mundane reality that is so difficult to deal with. If we could simply demonize the enemy—as so many seek to do, on all sides—then it would be simple to eradicate evil, to actually have a "war on terror" that could somehow be won. But such demonization will not give us a sufficient account of the violence of our existence. Just this Lenten season, on Ash Wednesday, just down the street from my home, a mother—the pastor of a local congregation of Baptists—administered the cruciform ashes to her nine-year-old daughter's forehead and then gently touched her nose. I do not know the words she spoke to her nine-year-old parishioner. But the traditional words, of course, are "Remember you are dust, and to dust you will return."

Within three hours, that dear child was killed—she who loved her friends and nature and animals and the goodness of God's creation—when a deer, running across the highway, burst through the windshield, passed into the backseat of the car, and killed this little one of God. All our community grieved together, and there were no words sufficient, no entity that could be demonized. This is a reality to which the crucifixion of Jesus attests: there is no enemy who can be simply demonized, thus violently destroyed, and righteousness thus established.

A True Story to Live By

Good Friday does not answer our questions of "why?" It does not answer why a beloved nine-year-old dies such a tragic death or why five-year-olds die of preventable disease and starvation that could be significantly reduced with the money wealthy countries spend on diet pills. It does not explain why one group of people would see another group of people as less than human, or as rightly torturable, or as the legitimate target of weapons of mass destruction. It does not explain why bad things happen to good people.

But it does give us a true story to live by: that even unto death, we may love and give and share and forgive. And that our doing so does *not* guarantee that we will "win" in the short run. It may, in fact, mean that we get ourselves killed. But the Jesus story also means that suffering love triumphs over violent hatred, that patience waits not forever for vindication, and that faith gives way to sight—which is also to say that Good Friday precedes Easter Sunday, in which the suffering love of God overcomes all the powers of darkness and death and oppression. Thus Jürgen Moltmann states that "even Auschwitz is in God himself....God in Auschwitz and Auschwitz in the crucified God—that is the basis for a real hope which both embraces and overcomes the world, and the ground for a love which is stronger than death and can sustain death."[6]

The New Testament is insistent that Good Friday is part of the story that we are also called to embody: "Whoever does not carry the cross and follow me cannot be my disciple" (Luke 14:27). "May I never boast of anything except the cross of our Lord Jesus Christ, by which the world has been crucified to me, and I to the world. . . . From now on, let no one make trouble for me; for I carry the marks of Jesus branded on my body" (Gal. 6:14, 17). "For to this you have been called, because Christ also suffered for you, leaving you an example, so that you should follow in his steps" (1 Pet. 2:21).

Thus, we come to this ironic observation, that while the Muslim may deny the historical fact of the crucified Jesus, we Christians have often denied the ethical relevance of the crucified Jesus. When the Crusader marked with the cross cleaves the skull of the infidel, when the conquistador bears the "Good News" to the New World as he slaughters and kidnaps the natives, and when the American Christian dangles a cross from the end of the machine gun with which he kills Muslims, he denies the crucified Jesus too.

The conquistador or the American Christian would deny, of course, any such denial, claiming that he cleaves, or slaughters, or shoots not with regard to "religion" but with regard to the "secular" order, or some such division of the world into two parts, one part in which the ethic of the cross is seen as authoritative, and one part in which the ethic of the sword is seen as authoritative. Thus, the Crusader who cleaves the skull of the infidel does not merely cleave a skull, but the world. The president who prays in private and makes war in public cleaves many skulls, but also the universe. Or perhaps it is more accurate to say that they *attempt* to cleave the world, to cleave the universe. We Christians have made good attempts at cleaving the universe into the "spiritual" and the "secular." But God's world will not be divided into two. It is God's world—all of it—and there is not a single secular molecule in it.[7] We Western Christians would do well to learn that from Muslims. And given that we claim to follow a crucified Messiah instead of Muhammad, the implications of that realization may be even more frightening for us Christians than that realization is for Muslims.

So, the Qur'anic refutation of a crucified Jesus may prompt offense on the part of the Christian. But that same Christian may simultaneously deny the "narrative logic" of the crucified Jesus by making war. In such a case, the Muslim at least is more honest, the Christian more duplicitous, with regard to the cross. That is to say, when the crucified Jesus becomes yet one more "doctrine" merely to be believed, stripped of its narrative force, stripped of its ethical significance for the disciple of that Jesus; when it becomes an otherworldly idea or transaction, as opposed to a historical encounter with the power of rebellion; when the cross becomes an emblem, or the Scriptures that testify to this Jesus become the morale booster to go off and kill the enemy whom Jesus commanded us to love; then the Christian has denied the crucified Jesus every bit as much as the Muslim has, but less honorably so.

So perhaps, with regard to the crucified Messiah, we might best summarize this way:

The Muslim denies with his words,
    because of what the Qur'an says;
the Christian denies with his deeds,
    despite what the Bible says.

20

The Arab Barbershop,
Changing Neighborhoods,
and Other Small Exercises in Courage

I did wonder, when the Arab Muslim held a straight razor to my neck, whether he hated all Americans. But first, some background.

In the *souks* of the Old City of Jerusalem—the ancient marketplaces hidden in cobblestoned and overcrowded alleyways and paths—one finds all sorts of delights for the senses: merchants selling nuts and dates and spices, butcher shops offering beef and lamb and chicken, rug salesmen especially eager to get a bit of one's time. I wandered many days in those colorful and loud and occasionally intimidating stone corridors and marketplaces, a feast of sights and sounds and smells. From early in my sojourn there, I wanted to get a haircut from an Arab barber in the souks of the Old City. So near the end of my stay, when my hair had gotten long, and my tan deep enough that the security forces had begun to stop me to see what passport I was carrying, I made my way to the barbershop.

The Hadith TV channel played, recounting the hadiths—the stories about Muhammad that carry great authoritative weight for the

Muslim community. My Arab barber seemed to speak little English, and I even less Arabic, but I sufficiently communicated my coiffure wishes and sat and enjoyed some time to rest in the barber's chair, one of those very fine pleasures in life. But I found that when the straight razor came out, my mind jumped to a murder mystery I had picked up in the reading room at Tantur, whose plot involved a psychopath jamming a Swiss Army knife into the necks of her victims. From the Swiss Army knife my mind raced to the straight razor moving toward my neck, and then to the thought, "I hope this guy doesn't hate Americans."

Turns out he gave me a beard trim that I now consider the epitome of a fine beard trim. I have not yet found a barber, nor have I found myself, able to reach the same fine style.

When he was done with my cut, trim, and shave, I arose from the barber's chair, so preoccupied with myself I had not realized that the other barber was no longer barbering but had unrolled his prayer mat, had his head bowed to the floor, and was praying behind us.

"Courage," it has been said, "is fear that has said its prayers."

Some years ago I completed giving an exam, and two of my students remained behind to chat. One of the students, a young woman, shared in the course of conversation that she had moved into a neighborhood where one of her friends was unwilling to spend the night. "Where did you move?" I asked. She told me: an ethnically diverse neighborhood, riddled with drug problems and economic difficulties. "Why did you move there?" I asked. She told me how she had recently been the victim of an attempted abduction; she had been jogging, a car of young men had stopped to ask her directions, she had tried to help them, and next thing she knew, one of the young men was trying to drag her into the car. She was able to kick and scream and get away, thank God.

After a bit, "So what does that have to do with you moving?" I asked.

"I found myself fearful," she replied, fearful whenever she found herself around people of the same ethnic background of the people who had attacked her. "I decided I did not want to live in fear, so I moved into a neighborhood where I would be forced to face my fear."

Oh, to have such courage.

It only recently occurred to me after years of teaching ethics courses that my teaching is a waste of time if either I or my students have no courage—that is, a willingness to suffer on behalf of what we believe to be right or true. And the only way to become a courageous person, Aristotle taught us, is by doing courageous deeds. Or, we should add, by the gift of God's Spirit; but my religious experience is more akin to the variety identified by William James as the slow and gradual kind that requires practice and deeds in order for the inner self to be transformed.

Thus the need to practice courage. This is one reason I encourage my students to do things that make them uncomfortable, to put themselves in uncomfortable contexts, so that they might exercise courage. In one class, for example, we practice "intentional conversations," in which I assign them a given topic and require that they engage in conversation on that topic in potentially difficult circumstances: to select someone—a random stranger in a coffee shop, a family member, or a professor or university administrator they find intimidating—with whom they assume they will have a fundamental disagreement, and then approach that person, tell them what they think, and, when that person replies to the contrary, say flatly, "I think you are wrong."

So, I need to regularly speak up when it makes me uncomfortable, to speak on behalf of someone being slandered, to tell the truth when it is not wanted, to acknowledge my fear of conflict. And I need to learn more good stories to tell—of Francis of Assisi, who embodied the notion of seeking first to understand rather than to be understood, by traveling in poverty and without arms in the midst of one of the Crusades to visit the sultan; of Dorothy Day, who refused to bend the knee to the federal authorities; of Martin Luther King Jr., who, after his house had been bombed and his life threatened, discovered a personal relationship with God that allowed him to keep standing up, speaking out, and putting one foot in front of the other in pursuit of the kingdom of God.

Ironically, just after a midmorning break while writing this chapter, I wandered into Alumni Auditorium, where the Nashville Symphony—dislocated from their beautiful Schermerhorn Symphony Center after the great Nashville flood of 2010—was rehearsing for an upcoming performance on our campus. Felix Mendelssohn's Fourth Symphony has not changed in centuries. The notes on the page remain the same; new editions may alter some notes, but the melody remains much the same. Yet here was a stage full of world-class musicians, under the direction of a guest conductor, rehearsing and practicing a piece they had undoubtedly played numerous times, the conductor coaching, coaxing, and prodding, insisting that a given passage evoke—he searched for the word—"joy."

Both the Qur'an and the Bible are like Mendelssohn's piece, in that the basic text has not changed much in the intervening centuries. But an element of performance is still required, and practice is necessary to perform well. The symphony orchestra is more like the biblical literalist, sticking more closely to the written notes, while jazz is perhaps less rigid but still bounded by the melody, and akin to other sorts of Bible or Qur'anic readings. In many ways, my argument in this book has been that the mainstream of Christianity, when it comes to war-making and peacemaking, has been playing a tune that is more akin to Muhammad's tune than to that of Jesus, even while claiming that Jesus's melody is superior. Or, more perversely, that too often the Christian performance has failed to get to the nobility of the Muhammad story, lacking its elegance and justice and equity.

I do not mean to say that I find the Muhammad story more convincing, elegant, or true than the Jesus story. I remain a follower of Jesus, deeply flawed and, so I suspect, not a very good follower. Frankly, I find the story of Jesus more compelling, provocative, and interesting. But even my new Muslim friends, I suspect, will not begrudge me this, but rather expect it of me.

What I find so very interesting about the Jesus story is precisely its difference from the Muhammad story: that victory and triumph come not through a simple historical victory over the powers of injustice through justifiable use of the sword, but through cross and resurrection. But this notion, I repeat, frightens me. I find the Muhammad logic very compelling: carefully, and with equity, retaliate against those who oppress and persecute. Justice, as well as love for oneself and one's neighbors, requires it. Yet the Jesus story proclaims that Jesus's faithfulness unto death—and the vindication of his faithfulness in the resurrection—prescribes a different way. And if we believe that story to be true, then it provides the antidote to our slavery and bondage to fear. The fearmongering of the media should be seen, for example, for what it is: a flat-footed denial of the story of Jesus. The fearmongering of talk-radio hosts who seek to galvanize an audience and improve their ratings should be seen for what it is: a flat-footed denial of the story of Jesus. The fearmongering of politicians who galvanize the citizenry to support a preemptive war, for using fear of what someone may someday do, should be seen for what it is: a flat-footed denial of the story of Jesus.

As Hebrews 2 puts it: "Since, therefore, the children share flesh and blood, [Jesus] himself likewise shared the same things, so that through death he might destroy the one who has the power of death, that is, the devil, and free those who all their lives were held in slavery by the fear of death" (vv. 14–15). If death has been defeated through suffering love and resurrection, then we who also love in this way, and potentially suffer in this way, need neither be enslaved by fear nor propagate fear. We need fear no man and no thing, except God alone, who has exhibited such great love for us that we are now called sons and daughters of God.

I have many good brothers and sisters in Jesus who are convinced, nonetheless, of the legitimacy of the Christian Just War tradition. Of course, they may be right. I once read, as I recollect, that Woodrow Wilson said that if you don't know somewhere in the back of your mind that you may be wrong, then you're an idiot. I do not *want* to be an idiot, so I try often to remind myself that I may be awfully wrong. But then again, humility like this prompts yet one more reason to be extremely cautious about employing war on behalf of what one believes to be true. It seems an act of great confidence, if not arrogance, to drop a bomb or strafe a village or enact the Powell Doctrine of overwhelming force when so many civilians, inevitably killed in modern warfare, will suffer.

Then again, the advocate of the Just War tradition might insist that there are situations that are so clearly and explicitly grotesque abuses that the use of the sword is not only justified but also required for the believer. (Still, we might point out that Romans 13 and 1 Timothy 2 assume that something like "police force" is an "ordained" part of the social order, but not something ordained for the follower of the crucified Messiah.) Frankly, I *want* to believe

152

what my Just Warrior brothers and sisters say—but I just cannot square it with the Jesus story.

In any case, another point I have tried to make clearly is this: it is *not* the careful and honest application of the JWT that troubles me most in American culture. The JWT often gets used as a tool of rationalization, and before we know it, the coherent, rigorous, and logical constraints of the JWT have become a pawn to rationalize the widespread destruction of water systems and infrastructure, or firebombing and atom-bombing, or going to war upon paltry grounds in the name of defending our "way of life." So, to my brothers and sisters who say they believe in the Christian Just War tradition, I plead with you: take the tradition seriously, apply it rigorously, and remember that all the principalities and powers, bent upon their own survival, often lie and justify and rationalize and seek to get us all to serve their vested interests.

Those who find their understanding of "love of neighbor" requiring something like the JWT can serve an immensely positive role in peacemaking in our world: what if, for example, as Glen Stassen asks us, the good Baptist Harry Truman, who wanted to take the Sermon on the Mount seriously, had been taught that the JWT absolutely prohibits the bombing of civilians?[1] What if military personnel who claim the lordship of Jesus are taught that there is an authority beyond the state, and that the JWT requires careful discernment about the justice of declaring war? What if Christian civilians, who desire to be supportive of their nation, are taught virtues that allow them to love their country while still practicing careful discernment in their assessment of national policies that too often lead to oppression and death?

Wherever we Christians come out upon the question of "pacifism" or "just war," we all will need immense courage to speak up and speak out: against nationalism and militarism, against fearmongering and hatred of enemies, against praying for "our troops" instead of praying for peace. We desperately need to learn to talk to people who are different from us, who have profound convictions that stand at deep odds with our own, to sit down at the table with them, to share coffee with them, to drink tea with them, to listen to their stories and their experiences, to extend hospitality rather than mere tolerance. We desperately need courage to engage peacemaking, in our families, neighborhoods, and communities; to desist from fearmongering; to stop forwarding the hateful emails that mock and presuppose the worst about our perceived enemies; to find ways to welcome the alien and foreigner as honored guest, instead of fearing that "they" will destroy our "way of life," for if we are living in bondage to fear, then we have already lost the "way of life" to which a cruciform Messiah calls us; to stop counting the United States, for all the many things about this country we may savor and know to be genuinely good, as the savior of the world, for the world already has a Savior; to stop the foolish rhetoric that speaks as if the United States government were the source of our liberties, for the American forefathers did not invent freedom.

Freedom is the gift of God and is enabled by cross and resurrection, not by the United States' Constitution, or Declaration of Independence, or well-intentioned and honorable soldiers. It is Jesus who gives us freedom, a freedom grounded in a willingness to love our enemies, to be willing to suffer and not retaliate in kind, to give food and drink and good to those who do ill to us. I am not saying that I have ever, to the degree that I have practiced it, found any of that easy. I am simply saying that this is the logic of the Jesus story. And any "freedoms" secured otherwise cannot, in the final analysis, be a freedom specified by that story.

O good and gracious God, grant us freedom that loves such as this.

Notes

Preface

1. Bob Smietana and Kate Howard, "Is Islam a Threat to America?," *Tennessean*, December 6, 2009, www.tennessean.com/apps/pbcs.dll/article?AID=2009912060340.

2. He reports that he counted texts in the Qur'an, the hadith, and the Sira, which is Muhammad's biography, and he apparently employed the version by Ibn Ishaq.

3. Though I suspect he was unaware of the extensive contemporary New Testament studies that indicate that Roman imperialism was a key contextual concern to the New Testament writers. If this is true, and the sort of reading I suggest of the New Testament below is accurate, then it turns out that in many ways the New Testament is concerned with war-making but is posing an alternative to the war-making, an alternative to the Pax Romana of the ancient world.

4. Several years of study of Islam does not an "expert" make. If you are looking for a historical introduction to Islam, there are many helpful resources. These include: John Esposito, "Great World Religions: Islam," from The Great Courses (Chantilly, VA: The Teaching Company, 2003), available at www.teach12.com/tgc/courses/course_detail.as px?cid=6102; Esposito and Dalia Mogahed, *Who Speaks for Islam? What a Billion Muslims Really Think* (New York: Gallup Press, 2007); Karen Armstrong, *Islam: A Short History* (New York: Modern Library, 2000); Malise Ruthven, *Islam: A Very Short Introduction* (New York: Oxford University Press, 1997); and Roland Machatschke, *The Basics: Islam* (Valley Forge, PA: Trinity Press International, 1997).

Chapter 1 The Muslim Enemy

1. I am not interested in arguing over what was intended by the reporter, nor in doing any exegesis on the newspaper article. I assumed then, and have continued to assume, goodwill on her part. The article is archived at www.tennessean.com/apps/pbcs.dll /article?AID=/20061129/NEWS06/611290429. The *Tennessean* graciously offered to allow me to print an unedited response piece the following day. Unfortunately, it was not read as widely as the front-page piece the previous day. Alas. See Lee C. Camp, "Theologian Disputes How Article Described His Thought," *Tennessean*, November 30, 2006, local edition, sec. B-3. It is available online at http://pqasb.pqarchiver.com/tennessean/access/1748516831.html

?FMT=ABS&FMTS=ABS:FT&date=Nov+30%2C+2006&author=LEE+CAMP&pub
=The+Tennessean&edition=&startpage=B.3&desc=Theologian+disputes+how+article
+described+his+talk.

2. http://littlegreenfootballs.com/article/23497_Tennessee_Dhimmitude_Watch
/comments/#ctop.

Chapter 2 To Seek to Understand Rather Than to Be Understood

1. Text taken from "A Prayer Attributed to St. Francis," in The (Online) Book of Common Prayer (under "Prayers and Thanksgivings"), www.bcponline.org.

2. Alan Jacobs, *A Theology of Reading: The Hermeneutics of Love* (Boulder, CO: Westview, 2001).

3. Miroslav Volf, *Exclusion and Embrace: A Theological Exploration of Identity, Otherness, and Reconciliation* (Nashville: Abingdon, 1996), 213. Throughout this section, I am indebted to Volf's discussion of this method in *Exclusion and Embrace*.

4. Volf puts it well: our task is not simply to affirm plurality, as if any one view of justice is as good as another. Instead, we must affirm what we believe to be true, must affirm and *act* upon what we believe to be just. But we must, simultaneously, "nurture an awareness of our own *fallibility*" (218). Of much import, James Wm. McClendon Jr. identifies the "principle of fallibility" as one of the two "constitutive rules" for doing theology in a third stream of Christianity, alongside Catholicism and Protestantism, the so-called baptist (little "b") or "Believers' Church" strand. See McClendon, *Ethics*, vol. 1, *Systematic Theology* (Nashville: Abingdon, 1986), 45.

5. This is, by now, a commonplace. My most recent favorite, well-nuanced, though now two-decades-old treatment of such themes is Lesslie Newbigin's *The Gospel in a Pluralist Society* (Grand Rapids: Eerdmans, 1989).

6. Volf, *Exclusion and Embrace*, 215.

7. McClendon, *Ethics*, 45–46.

8. The "sin" that Paul here sees as the common sin of humanity is worshiping created things instead of the Creator. "They exchanged the glory of the immortal God for images resembling a mortal human being or birds or four-footed animals or reptiles. . . . They exchanged the truth about God for a lie and worshiped and served the creature rather than the Creator, who is blessed for ever!" (Rom. 1:23, 25). My reading of this text is indebted to Richard Hays, *The Moral Vision of the New Testament: A Contemporary Introduction to New Testament Ethics* (San Francisco: HarperSanFrancisco, 1996), 389.

9. But is there time for such reflection when manifest injustice is occurring? Is there time to reflect upon the understanding of the enemy when the enemy is perpetrating horror? Perhaps this is but another ivory tower indulgence? A practice good for academics and those who live in suburbia, but not so good for those experiencing the daily onslaught of oppression? Volf notes that Scripture calls us not so much to mull over "justice" as to do justice (see Hos. 12:6; Amos 5:15, 24; Mic. 6:8; Isa. 58:6). Our reflection must always serve the end of doing justice. Double vision cannot simply be something done prior to the struggle for justice, but must be in the midst of the struggle for justice. The reason for this is simple: "The fiercer the struggle against the injustice you suffer, the blinder you will be to the injustice you inflict, " observes Volf, *Exclusion and Embrace*, 217. Indeed, as I was reminded in my digging through the pages of Christian history, the holier the rhetoric, the more confident the conviction, the greater the temptation to violent and bloody crusade. As numerous wise ones have observed, we become what we hate. Practicing double vision might enable us to avoid falling prey to such hatred and bigotry.

10. Roland Bainton, *Christian Attitudes toward War and Peace: A Historical Survey and Critical Re-evaluation* (1960; repr., Nashville: Abingdon, 1990), 112–13.

11. Ibid., 147, 151.

Chapter 3 Looking for New Testament Christianity

1. Here, I particularly refer to the exegetical work of Walter Wink that has become popular in the last two decades. Walter Wink, *Naming the Powers: The Language of Power in the New Testament* (Minneapolis: Fortress Press, 1984); *Unmasking the Powers: The Invisible Forces That Determine Human Existence* (Minneapolis: Fortress Press, 1986); *Engaging the Powers: Discernment and Resistance in a World of Domination* (Minneapolis: Fortress Press, 1992); and most recently abridged into *The Powers That Be: Theology for a New Millennium* (New York: Doubleday, 1998).

2. See Tolbert Fanning, "To His Excellency the President of The Confederate States of America," full text in Earl West, *The Life and Times of David Lipscomb* (Germantown, TN: Religious Book Service, 1987), 87–89; Michael W. Casey, "The Closing of Cordell Christian College: A Microcosm of American Intolerance during World War I," *Chronicles of Oklahoma* 76 (Spring 1998): 20–37; and Michael Casey, "The Courage of Conscience: The Conscientious Objectors of World War II and the Churches of Christ" (unpublished lecture, presented to the Christian Scholars' Conference at Lipscomb University, Nashville, TN, July 19, 1991).

Chapter 4 The Early Church and the Jesus Story

1. Roland Bainton, *Christian Attitudes toward War and Peace: A Historical Survey and Critical Re-evaluation* (1960; repr., Nashville: Abingdon, 1990), 53.

2. Text appears as "Acts of Saint Maximilian the Martyr," in *War and the Christian Conscience: From Augustine to Martin Luther King, Jr.*, ed. Albert Marrin (Chicago: Henry Regnery, 1971), 40–43.

3. Bainton, *Christian Attitudes*, 53.

4. Ibid., 66; and John Driver, *How Christians Made Peace with War: Early Christian Understandings of War*, Peace and Justice Series 2 (Scottdale, PA: Herald Press, 1988), 23, 26. Driver limits the period of pacifist writers to the dates 150–250 (26). I am indebted throughout much of this chapter to Bainton's examination, "The Pacifism of the Early Church," in *Christian Attitudes*, 66–84.

5. Lisa Sowle Cahill, *Love Your Enemies: Discipleship, Pacifism, and Just War Theory* (Minneapolis: Fortress Press, 1994), 55.

6. Bainton, *Christian Attitudes*, 73.

7. Athenagoras, *A Plea for Christians* 35, trans. B. P. Pratten, in *The Ante-Nicene Fathers*, ed. Alexander Roberts and James Donaldson (1885; repr., Peabody, MA: Hendrickson, 2004), 2:147. *Ante-Nicene Fathers* and *Nicene and Post-Nicene* volumes are online at www .ccel.org/fathers.html.

8. Tertullian, *Apology* 30, trans. S. Thelwall, in *Ante-Nicene Fathers* 3:42.

9. Ibid.

10. Tertullian, *Apology* 31, in *Ante-Nicene Fathers* 3:42.

11. Tertullian, *Apology* 32, in *Ante-Nicene Fathers* 3:42–43.

12. Tertullian, *Apology* 37, in *Ante-Nicene Fathers* 3:45.

13. Tertullian, *On Idolatry* 19, in *Early Christians Speak: Faith and Life in the First Three Centuries*, ed. and trans. Everett Ferguson, 3rd ed. (Abilene, TX: ACU Press, 1999), 216. The text is obscured at the word *unbelted* in *Ante-Nicene Fathers* 3:73.

14. Tertullian, *The Chaplet, or De Corona* 11, trans. S. Thelwall, in *Ante-Nicene Fathers* 3:99.

15. Bainton, *Christian Attitudes*, 77.

16. Athenagoras, *Plea for the Christians* 11, in *Ante-Nicene Fathers* 2:134.

17. Justin Martyr, *Dialogue with Trypho* 110, trans. Alexander Roberts and James Donaldson, in *Ante-Nicene Fathers* 1:254. Justin continues, "And we cultivate piety, righteousness, philanthropy, faith, and hope, which we have from the Father Himself through Him who was crucified; and sitting each under his vine, i.e., each man possessing his own married wife."

18. Justin Martyr, *The First Apology of Justin* 39, trans. Alexander Roberts and James Donaldson, in *Ante-Nicene Fathers* 1:176.

19. Clement of Alexandria, *Exhortation to the Heathen* 10, in *Ante-Nicene Fathers* 2:202.

20. Cyprian, *The Treatises of Cyprian*, "Treatise 9. On the Advantage of Patience §16," trans. Ernest Wallis, in *Ante-Nicene Fathers* 5:488.

21. Cyprian, *The Epistles of Cyprian*, "Epistle 1. To Donatus §6," trans. Ernest Wallis, in *Ante-Nicene Fathers* 5:277; and *The Treatises of Cyprian*, "Treatise 2. On the Dress of Virgins §11," in *Ante-Nicene Fathers* 5:433. See also Bainton, *Christian Attitudes*, 73.

22. Dionysius of Alexandria, *Works of Dionysius—Extant Fragments*, "Epistle 14—From His Fourth Festival Epistle," trans. S. D. F. Salmond, in *Ante-Nicene Fathers* 6:110.

23. Justin Martyr, *First Apology* 15, in *Ante-Nicene Fathers* 1:167.

24. Arnobius, *The Seven Books of Arnobius Against the Heathen: Adversus Gentes* 1:6, trans. Hamilton Bryce and Hugh Campbell, in *Ante-Nicene Fathers* 6:415.

25. Thieleman J. van Braght, ed., *The Bloody Theater; or, Martyrs' Mirror of the Defenseless Christians*, trans. Joseph F. Sohm (1660; Scottdale, PA: Herald Press, 1950), 416.

26. Ibid., 417.

Chapter 5 The New Testament and the Politics of Jesus

1. Quoted in Walter Wink, *Engaging the Powers: Discernment and Resistance in a World of Domination* (Minneapolis: Fortress Press, 1992), 216. Also in Dale W. Brown, *Biblical Pacifism*, 2nd ed. (Nappanee, IN: Evangel, 2003), 5, 62–63.

2. Especially those influenced by the intellectual strand descending from Max Weber and Ernst Troeltsch.

3. Compare the almost identical language in 1 Thess. 5:15.

4. Some important works in this regard: John Howard Yoder, *The Politics of Jesus: Vicit Agnus Noster*, 2nd ed. (Grand Rapids: Eerdmans, 1994); Richard B. Hays, *The Moral Vision of the New Testament: Community, Cross, New Creation: A Contemporary Introduction to New Testament Ethics* (San Francisco: HarperSanFrancisco, 1996); Lisa Sowle Cahill, *Love Your Enemies: Discipleship, Pacifism, and Just War Theory* (Minneapolis: Fortress Press, 1994); and Paul Ramsey, *The Just War: Force and Political Responsibility* (1968; repr., Lanham, MD: Rowman & Littlefield, 1983).

5. Wink, *Engaging the Powers*, 217.

6. This is not only a concern in Pauline writings but is also a major concern of the book of Acts.

7. Donald Durnbaugh's classic work *The Believers' Church: The History and Character of Radical Protestantism* (Scottdale, PA: Herald Press, 1985), especially pp. 242–63, is a helpful guide here. For those movements that were forged in the midst of persecution by the governing authorities, such as the Mennonites and other heirs of the sixteenth-century radical Protestant Reformation, the stance has tended to be more distance from participation in the work of government. For movements that nonetheless hold to nonviolence but were forged

in a less coercive environment, such as the Quakers, there has tended to be less distance from participation in the work of government. I do not mean or imply here that "nonparticipation" in governmental offices or roles is expected or required by Christian discipleship. I do mean to say that, if we do so participate, we do so as disciples of the way of Jesus, and not as functionaries of a state who, while serving that state, set aside the way of Jesus.

8. See John Howard Yoder, *The Christian Witness to the State* (Eugene, OR: Wipf and Stock, 1998).

Chapter 6 The Qur'an and the Politics of Muhammad

1. Alfred Guillaume, *The Life of Muhammad*, a translation of Muhammad Ibn Ishāq's *Sīrat Rasūl Allāh* (Karachi: Oxford University Press, 1955), 143.

2. Marmaduke Pickthall, *The Meaning of the Glorious Koran* (New York: Alfred A. Knopf, 1982), 675; see sura 111: "The power of Abû Lahab will perish. . . . He will be plunged in flaming fire."

3. William Montgomery Watt, introduction to ibid., xiii.

4. One cannot, however, simply add 622 to an Islamic date to get the Western calendar year, as the Islamic year is reckoned on a lunar basis, with a year comprising 354 days instead of 365.

5. Though Seyyid Qutb, seen by many as the father of contemporary militant Islam, considers this merely a strategic command: retaliation would have been useless and would have led to the demise of the nascent Muslim community. See Seyyid Qutb, *Milestones* (Damascus: Dar al-Ilm, n.d.), 76.

6. Guillaume, *Life of Muhammad*, 212–13.

7. Louay M. Safi, *Peace and the Limits of War: Transcending the Classical Conception of Jihad* (Washington, DC: International Institute of Islamic Thought, 2003), 20.

8. The text of the covenant is in the appendix of Safi, 40–41. Mustafa Abu Sway notes that "in the biographies of the Prophet (Books of Sirah), the covenant in the original Arabic says that the Jews form 'one Ummah' along with the Muslims. It is beautiful language." Personal correspondence, September 2010.

9. John Kelsay, *Arguing the Just War in Islam* (Cambridge, MA: Harvard University Press, 2007), 25.

10. I explore this at some length in "'Let Every Soul Be Subject': Romans 13 and Christian Pacifism," in *A Faith Not Worth Fighting For* (forthcoming, Cascade Books, 2011). See also Oscar Cullman, "Paul and The State" in *The State In The New Testament* (New York: Scribner, 1956).

11. Though it is not yet clear to me what the phrase "religion is all for Allah" means in this context.

12. Kelsay, *Arguing the Just War*, 97, emphasis added.

13. The powers that wield policelike force still have their place as agents under God's ordering and providence—to check violence—but this is not the vocation of those who have submitted themselves to the lordship of the crucified Messiah. The classic New Testament texts on this point are Romans 13 and 1 Timothy 2. On Romans 13, John Howard Yoder's treatment in his chapter in *The Politics of Jesus: Vicit Agnus Noster*, 2nd ed. (Grand Rapids: Eerdmans, 1994), remains most instructive; while William Stringfellow's *Conscience and Obedience: The Politics of Romans 13 and Revelation 13 in Light of the Second Coming* (1977; repr., Eugene, OR: Wipf and Stock, 2004), is likewise a classic that challenges a reading of Romans 13 that proceeds from a conservative status quo hermeneutic.

Chapter 7 On the Christian, the Old Testament, and War

1. Peter C. Craigie, *The Problem of War in the Old Testament* (1978; repr., Grand Rapids: Eerdmans, 1981).

2. In fact, one finds insistent critique of militarism in the prophets. Dependence upon the might of arms and foreign alliances was but one more manifestation of idolatrous unfaithfulness. See, for example, Isaiah 31: "Alas for those who go down to Egypt for help and who rely on horses, who trust in chariots because they are many" (v. 1).

3. See John Driver, *How Christians Made Peace with War: Early Christian Understandings of War*, Peace and Justice Series 2 (Scottdale, PA: Herald Press, 1988), 21–22.

4. Celsus cited by Origen, *Origen against Celsus* 8:68, trans. Frederick Crombie, in *The Ante-Nicene Fathers*, ed. Alexander Roberts and James Donaldson (1885; repr., Peabody, MA: Hendrickson, 2004), 4:665.

Chapter 8 The Early Muslims and the Muhammad Story

1. John Kelsay, *Arguing the Just War in Islam* (Cambridge, MA: Harvard University Press, 2007), 97, says the same with regard to Islam: a notion of justifiable war is "an aspect of the foundational narrative of Islam." Throughout this chapter I rely heavily upon Kelsay (2007) as well as his earlier work, *Islam and War: A Study in Comparative Ethics* (Louisville: Westminster John Knox, 1993).

2. Gandhi, "My Jail Experiences XI [Continued]: What I Read—2," in *The Collected Works of Mahatma Gandhi* (New Delhi: Publications Division, Government of India, 1999), 29:133, available at www.gandhiserve.org/cwmg/VOL029.PDF.

3. Jane Idleman Smith, *Muslims, Christians, and the Challenge of Interfaith Dialogue* (New York: Oxford University Press, 2007), 27.

4. Kelsay, *Islam and War*, 33–34.

5. Ibid., 34.

6. Cited in ibid.

7. Though I would note in passing that this seems to be a significant difference between classical Islam and classical Christianity: that while Christianity can use language that entails the motif of struggle, and while much moralistic Christian teaching talks as if we may simply "choose" to do God's will, "surrender" of one's will turns out to be a better antidote than "struggle," especially if one takes seriously the insight of the apostle Paul: that the means by which we overcome the slavery to the power of sin is through *surrender* of ourselves to the will of God, instead of a *struggle*, no matter how noble, with the power of sin itself. (See Rom. 6–8.)

8. Kelsay, *Islam and War*, 35.

9. From Majid Khadduri, trans., *The Islamic Law of Nations: Shaybani's Siyar* (Baltimore: Johns Hopkins University Press, 1966), 75–77, cited in Kelsay, *Arguing the Just War*, 100–101.

10. Kelsay, *Arguing the Just War*, 100ff.

11. Louay M. Safi, *Peace and the Limits of War: Transcending the Classical Conception of Jihad* (Washington, DC: International Institute of Islamic Thought, 2003), 37–38.

12. Ibid., 1.

13. Ibid., 1–2.

14. Ibid., 2.

15. Following Kelsay's translation, *Arguing the Just War*, 107.

16. Khadduri, *Islamic Law of Nations*, 101–2, cited in Kelsay, *Arguing the Just War*, 107.

17. Kelsay, *Arguing the Just War*, 130ff.

Chapter 9 The Constantine Story and the Christian Just War Tradition

1. John Howard Yoder, *Discipleship as Political Responsibility* (Scottdale, PA: Herald Press, 1964), 44–45. Says Yoder: "The Christian who wants to put the role of Christian living into second place in order to serve the state as a first priority is like a musician who leaves the stage in order to work as an usher in the concert hall. Of course the usher is also necessary; but the musician cannot be replaced in his or her role. And musicians, of all people, should know that they are of most value when they perform the role that no one else can fill. If the musician is not on stage, and there is therefore no concert, then the usher's role has no meaning either."

2. By "formally," I mean the overarching logic of the position. Often in the field of ethics, one might speak of the "formal shape" of an argument, referring to the root logic. The "concrete shape" or the "particular shape" refers more to the actual content of the particulars of the argument. In the case here, the formal shape is the same: war is regrettable and to be avoided, but it is sometimes necessary in administering justice and seeking to establish a just political order. Moreover, in some particulars, the content is the same: for example, both the Christian Just War tradition and the Muslim tradition of jihad claim that women and children should not be killed in war—that is, that civilians should not be directly targeted.

3. Cicero, *De Officiis* 1.11, trans. Walter Miller, *Loeb Classical Library: Cicero in Twenty-Eight Volumes* (Cambridge, MA: Harvard University Press, 1975), 21:35, 37, quoted in *War and the Christian Conscience: From Augustine to Martin Luther King, Jr.*, ed. Albert Marrin (Chicago: Henry Regnery, 1971), 40–43, 50.

4. Toby Keith, "Courtesy of the Red, White, and Blue," *Unleashed* (Nashville: Dreamworks, 2002).

5. Lisa Sowle Cahill, *Love Your Enemies: Discipleship, Pacifism, and Just War Theory* (Minneapolis: Fortress Press, 1994), 58.

6. Augustine, *The City of God* 4.4, trans. Marcus Dods, in *Nicene and Post-Nicene Fathers*, ed. Philip Schaff, 1st series (Buffalo: Christian Literature, 1887), 2:66.

7. St. Augustine, *The City of God* 4.4, 15; 19.7, in *Nicene and Post-Nicene Fathers*.

8. I summarize here from Yoder's unpublished, inductive study, "Conspectus of the Criteria of the Just War." See also John Howard Yoder, *When War Is Unjust: Being Honest in Just War Thinking*, 2nd ed. (Eugene, OR: Wipf and Stock, 2001); and Cahill, *Love Your Enemies*.

9. I recollect several who have said yes through the years—but I did not count their answers, because they had heard me teach or preach on the criteria. Other than those, I recollect only one other student who indicated some such moral instruction by the church.

10. So, for example, if in the case of the most recent Iraq war (most) honest adherents to the Just War tradition agreed (in this case) with the pacifists that the war in Iraq was illegitimate, what other commitments or convictions were at work? Professor Shaun Casey circulated a brief statement opposing the war, which was signed by numerous Christian ethicists who subscribed both to the Just War tradition and Christian pacifism. See "100 Leading Christian Ethicists Oppose Iraq War," at www.sojo.net/index.cfm?action=action. ethicists_statement. One important and noteworthy exception to my critique is the important new book by Daniel M. Bell Jr., *Just War as Christian Discipleship: Recentering the Tradition in the Church Rather Than the State* (Grand Rapids: Brazos Press, 2009), in which Bell argues that the Just War tradition must be recovered as a discipline of the church—instead of a tool of statecraft. And though I believe, in the end, that the Just War tradition is not a faithful expression of Christian discipleship, Bell's book and argument are both, nonetheless, very important and honorable, and it is the sort of work that the honest practitioners of the Just War tradition must do, and I hope they will continue to do, for they may thereby save many lives and sow seeds of nonviolent resolution to conflict.

11. Cahill, *Love Your Enemies*, 213.

12. Stanley Hauerwas, "Sacrificing the Sacrifice of War," (public lecture, Christ Church Cathedral, Nashville, TN, February 12, 2011).

Chapter 10 Crusading for Christ

1. Tamim Ansary, *Destiny Disrupted: A History of the World through Islamic Eyes* (New York: Public Affairs, 2009), 139; and Leona F. Cordery, "Cannibal Diplomacy: Otherness in the Middle English Text *Richard Coer de Lion*," in *Meeting the Foreign in the Middle Ages*, ed. Albrecht Classen (New York: Routledge, 2002), 156. Cordery argues that famine, and therefore severe hunger, played a part in the Franks' decision to eat their victims.

2. Amin Maalouf, *The Crusades through Arab Eyes*, trans. Jon Rothschild (New York: Schocken, 1985).

3. Ibid., xi.

4. Roland Bainton, *Christian Attitudes toward War and Peace: A Historical Survey and Critical Re-evaluation* (1960; repr., Nashville: Abingdon, 1990), 112.

5. Maalouf, *Crusades through Arab Eyes*, 38–39.

6. Ibid., 39. Maalouf also notes that one explanation for the cannibalism was the extreme conditions of famine, an explanation he finds unconvincing.

7. Ibid., xiv.

8. Ibid.

9. Cited in ibid., 1.

10. Steven Runciman, "The Pilgrimages to Palestine before 1095," in *A History of the Crusades*, vol. 1, ed. Marshall W. Baldwin (Philadelphia: University of Philadelphia Press, 1958), 78.

11. Maalouf, *Crusades through Arab Eyes*, 47.

12. Ibid., 50–51.

13. Ibid., 51.

14. Christopher Tyerman, *The Crusades: A Very Short Introduction* (New York: Oxford University Press, 2005), 7.

15. All cited in Manuel Percy-Rivas, "Bush Vows to Rid the World of 'Evil-Doers,'" *CNN.com*, September 16, 2001, http://edition.cnn.com/2001/US/09/16/gen.bush.terrorism/index.html.

16. Tyerman, *Crusades*, 22.

17. Ibid., 42–52.

18. James Turner Johnson, *The Holy War Idea in Western and Islamic Traditions* (University Park: Pennsylvania State University Press, 1997), 10–11.

Chapter 11 The Cowboy Museum

1. Some of the material in this chapter was previously published in Lee C. Camp, "Keeping Alive the Narratives of War and Peace," in *And the Word Became Flesh: Studies in History, Communication, and Scripture in Memory of Michael W. Casey*, ed. Thomas H. Olbricht and David Fleer (Eugene, OR: Pickwick, 2009), 269–83. Used by permission of the editors.

2. Dee Brown, *Bury My Heart at Wounded Knee: An Indian History of the American West* (New York: Holt, Rinehart & Winston, 1970), xxiii.

3. Here my storytelling follows Richard Drinnon, *Facing West: The Metaphysics of Indian-Hating and Empire-Building* (Norman: University of Oklahoma Press, 1997), 35ff.

4. John Underhill, *Newes from America . . . Containing a True Relation of Their War-like Proceedings These Two Years Last Past* (London, 1638), cited in Drinnon, *Facing West*, 36.

5. Ibid., 36 and 37. Drinnon goes on to incisively note: "Of course rulers eager to make war can make do with almost any first victim, so long as his death will infect everyone with the feeling of being threatened and provide basis for belief that 'the enemy,' broadly defined, is responsible. If this minimal foundation be laid, every other reason for his death may be ignored or suppressed, as Elias Canetti observed, save one, the victim's 'membership in the group to which one belongs oneself'" (38). Drinnon notes that the apparently innocent beginning to the war was, in fact, even less innocent than it appears: surely the death of a dozen Indians killed by Gallop could satisfy the thirst for vengeance for Oldham's death? Apparently not. How civilized, we might note, was Moses's limiting injunction of an eye for an eye and a tooth for a tooth compared to ancient Near Eastern thirst for blood, or (some of) the early Puritans' thirst for blood.

6. Cited in ibid., 42.

7. Ibid.

8. Ibid., 43. To reiterate: the point here is not that the Native Americans never indulged their bloodlust. It seems an all-too-common human practice, to give way to the lust for violence. Rather, the point is that the stories told placed the bloodlust all on the side of the "enemie." In fact, in the case of the Pequots, Drinnon's account is telling on this point: it appears that the "systematic ferocity of the Europeans" far outweighed that of their opponents. In fact, the Narragansett, allied with the Englishmen against the Pequots, came to Underhill after the battle and "cried Mach it, mach it; that is, It is naught, it is naught, because it is too furious, and slays too many men" (ibid., citing Underhill). In Underhill's professional estimation as an English soldier, the Indians fought "more for pastime, than to conquer and subdue enemies" (ibid.). In other words, in this case, the ferocious and systematic war-making of the Christian Europeans far outweighed the "hobby" of Indian war-making.

9. Ibid., 44, 45.

10. Ibid., 46.

11. Ibid., 47.

12. James Bradley, *Flyboys: A True Story of Courage* (New York: Little, Brown, 2003), 63ff.

13. Ibid., 66.

14. Ibid., 66–67. Bradley notes (68) that in a survey of the editors of 192 Christian publications, three alone believed Filipinos should be granted independence. The *Missionary Record* asked, "Has it ever occurred to you that Jesus was the most imperial of the imperialists?"

15. All cited in ibid., 68–72.

16. Cited in ibid., 71.

17. Cited in ibid., 37.

Chapter 12 The Western Tradition of Terror

1. I am unsure of the exact number the gentleman said; and there are a variety of reports on how many people were killed instantly in Hiroshima and Nagasaki, and how many were killed in the aftermath of radiation poisoning and cancers due to radiation.

2. Daniel M. Bell Jr., *Just War as Christian Discipleship: Recentering the Tradition in the Church Rather Than the State* (Grand Rapids: Brazos Press, 2009), 60. Bell incisively notes on p. 40: "When Sherman declared that war was hell, whatever he may have thought he was doing, he was not in fact making an accurate observation about the eternal and unchanging nature of war. He was not simply describing the way war must be, the way it always has been and always will be. Rather, he was, perhaps unwittingly, revealing much about his own moral, cultural, political, and military formation in a novel kind of warfare that was less restrained, more total, and less honorable than what preceded it. In other

words, it is not that Sherman and others like him discovered that war was hell; rather, they made it so. As Paul Ramsey puts it, 'War first became total in the minds of men.' War is a human practice that is as amenable to moral deformation and corruption as it is to moral guidance and limitation."

3. Cited by Lloyd Lewis, *Sherman: Fighting Prophet* (New York: Harcourt, Brace, 1932), 330.

4. See Ibid., 334–35. Sherman sent a letter to a major in Alabama to be read to the southern civilians, "so as to prepare them for my coming," in which he explained that "in Europe whence we derive our principles of war, wars are between kings or rulers through hired armies, and not between people. These remain as it were neutral and sell their produce to whatever army is in possession. . . . Therefore the general rule was and is that war is confined to the armies engaged and should not visit the houses of families or private interests." But the Civil War was a war of insurrection, Sherman insisted. "I believe this war is the result of false political doctrines for which we all as a people are responsible." That is, the people of the South had desired the war. "Very well," he replied: "A people who will persevere in war beyond a certain limit ought to know the consequence. Many, many people with less pertinacity have been wiped out of national existence." If they persist, they can expect great consequences: "To those who submit to rightful law and authority, all gentleness and forbearance; but to the petulant and persistent secessionists, why, death is mercy and the quicker he or she is disposed of the better.

"Satan and the rebellious saints of Heaven were allowed a continuous existence in hell merely to swell their just punishment. To such as would rebel against a Government so mild and just as ours was in peace, a punishment equal would not be unjust."

It would be unfair to see Sherman as a heartless monster bent upon as much senseless killing and death as possible, however. See John F. Marszalek, *Sherman's March to the Sea* (Abilene, TX: McWhiney Foundation Press, 2005). Marszalek maintains that Sherman employed "warfare of destructiveness" as a means "not to brutalize but to end the war as quickly as possible with the least loss of life" (14). Sherman's technique "was part of the development of modern warfare, the ascendance of the idea that war does not consist simply of armies fighting other armies on battlefields, but rather of societies battling each other through calculated destruction in order to break the other's will. Sherman's march to the sea was not the application of senseless brutality for its own sake; it was a well-planned attempt to break the will of the Confederacy and bring the Civil War to a more rapid end" (13–14). "Destroy rather than kill," says Marszalek, was Sherman's tactic (109). Influenced at West Point by the moral philosophy of James Kent, Sherman was introduced to the notion that war entails, says Marszalek, "a dissolution of morality and was fought not simply between two opposing armies but between two societies" (20). At one point in the war, Sherman would later proclaim—in great frustration with some of the immoral tactics of the Confederates—"when one nation is at war with another, all the people of one are enemies of the other." This being the case, Sherman thought it quite legitimate to "visit punishment upon the adherents of that cause which employs such agents" (23). Employing apocalyptic language of judgment, Sherman's wife, Ellen, proclaimed, "I hope this may be not only a war of emancipation but [also] of extermination & that all under the influence of the foul fiend may be driven like the Swine into the Sea. May we carry fire & sword into their states till not one habitation is left standing" (23–24).

My point here is that (a) this is the same logic that overthrows the classic restraints of JWT, which so many Just War theorists so rightly remind us, and that (b) this same logic is also employed by bin Laden (see below).

5. Marszalek, *Sherman's March to the Sea*, 26–27.

6. W. G. Sebald, *On the Natural History of Destruction*, trans. Anthea Bell (New York: Random House, 2003), 26–27.

7. Ibid., 28.

8. Ibid., 35.

9. Cited in ibid., 29.

10. Ibid., 15–17.

11. From Sir Charles Webster and Noble Frankland, *The Strategic Air Offensive against Germany* (London: Her Majesty's Stationery Office, 1954–56), 4:144, cited in ibid., 17.

12. Sebald, *On the Natural History of Destruction*, 17–18.

13. Cited in Gerard J. De Groot, "Why Did They Do It?" *Times Higher Educational Supplement*, October 16, 1992, 18, cited in ibid., 19.

14. Sebald, *On the Natural History of Destruction*, 3.

15. According to the teacher's supplement to the film *The Fog of War*, more than sixty Japanese cities were firebombed before the atomic bombs fell on Nagasaki and Hiroshima. See The Choices Program and the Critical Oral History Project, "The Teacher's Guide for *The Fog of War*: An Errol Morris Film," (Providence, RI: Watson Institute for International Studies, 2004), 4. Also available online at www.sonyclassics.com/fogofwar/_media/pdf/lesson PlanFOG.pdf. The firebombing of Tokyo alone on March 9, 1945, resulted in the deaths of between 90,000 and 100,000 people, and "another million were rendered homeless. Sixteen square miles were incinerated, and the glow of the flames was visible 150 miles away." Conrad C. Crane, "Toyko, Air Attack on (9–10 March 1945)," *PBS*, www.pbs.org/thewar/detail_5229 .htm. Errol Morris's film *The Fog of War* is a helpful case study to illustrate the manner in which utilitarian logic often trumps the rule-based limits of the Just War tradition. On the quote from McNamara, see textbox on p. 8 of the study guide.

16. Here I refer of course to the start of the most recent war in Iraq.

Chapter 13 Terrorism bin Laden Style

1. Osama bin Laden, "Full Text: Bin Laden's 'Letter to America,'" *Observer Worldview*, Sunday, November 24, 2002, under World News, www.guardian.co.uk/world/2002/nov/24 /theobserver, (Q1) section (3). Text can also be found in "To the Americans: October 6, 2002," *Messages to the World: The Statements of Osama Bin Laden*, ed. Bruce Lawrence (New York: Verso, 2005), 160–72.

2. John L. Esposito, *Unholy War: Terror in the Name of Islam* (New York: Oxford University Press, 2002), 3. My recounting of Osama bin Laden here largely follows Esposito.

3. PBS Frontline, "Interview: Osama bin Laden" (May 1998), *Frontline*, www.pbs.org wgbh/pages/frontline/shows/binladen/who/interview.html.

4. Ibid.

5. Osama bin Laden, "Letter to America," (Q1) section (3).

6. PBS Frontline, "Interview: Osama bin Laden."

7. Ibid.

8. John Miller's interview with bin Laden, available at ibid.

9. Bin Laden, "Letter to America," (Q1) section (3).

Chapter 14 Taking Stock

1. Thus, for example, it was reported that "vast crowds" of Iranians took to the streets after 9/11 to hold a prayer vigil for those slain in the unjust terrorist attacks. Gordon Corera, "Iran's Gulf of Misunderstanding with US," *BBC News*, September 25, 2006, http://news

.bbc.co.uk/2/hi/middle_east/5377914.stm; and "Islamic World Deplores US Losses," *BBC News*, September 14, 2001, http://news.bbc.co.uk/2/hi/americas/1544955.stm.

Chapter 15 Why "Religion" Is Not (Necessarily) the Problem

1. William T. Cavanaugh, *The Myth of Religious Violence: Secular Ideology and the Roots of Modern Conflict* (New York: Oxford University Press, 2009). Much of the following chapter is indebted to Cavanaugh's introduction and first chapter.

2. Charles Kimball, *When Religion Becomes Evil* (San Francisco: HarperSanFrancisco, 2002), 1.

3. Cavanaugh, *Myth of Religious Violence*, 61.

4. Ibid., 59.

5. Ibid., 56.

6. Talal Asad, *On Suicide Bombing* (New York: Columbia University Press, 2007), 62–63.

7. There is a renewed and expansive discussion on the doctrine of the atonement; I tend to agree with the critics of the Calvinist penal substitutionary doctrine of the atonement: its governing metaphor is not biblical, and it perverts, in my opinion, some of the fundamental trajectories of the biblical account.

8. Richard Gamble, *The War for Righteousness: Progressive Christianity, the Great War, and the Rise of the Messianic Nation* (Wilmington, DE: ISI, 2003), 5, cited in Asad, *On Suicide Bombing*, 86–87.

9. Gamble, *War for Righteousness*, 153, cited in Asad, 87.

Chapter 16 The Oklahoma Bombing, and Why America Can Never Commit Terrorist Acts

1. Kerry Noble, *Tabernacle of Hate: Why They Bombed Oklahoma City* (Prescott, ON: Voyageur, 1998).

2. See, for example, Daniel Levitas, *The Terrorist Next Door: The Militia Movement and the Radical Right* (New York: Thomas Dunne Books, 2002). "Gale's Posse manifesto fed and nurtured the American militia movement—including, in part, the ideology that motivated the Oklahoma City bombing orchestrated by Terry Nichols and Timothy McVeigh in 1995" (300).

3. Ibid., 1. "Arise and fight!" Gale said at another time. "If a Jew comes near you, run a sword through him" (cited in ibid., 2). Gale, along with numerous other right-wing groups like the CSA, adhered to the doctrine of Christian Identity, which claims that Anglo-Saxon Christians were the chosen people of God. The Identity doctrine follows an earlier teaching called British Israelism, in which the ten lost tribes of Israel purportedly made their way to Britain. Jews were children of the devil, while nonwhite races were "mud people," and thus all "race mixing" violated, proclaimed Gale and other Identity adherents, God's law.

4. James Corcoran, *Bitter Harvest: Gordon Kahl and the Posse Comitatus: Murder in the Heartland* (New York: Viking, 1990), 152–53.

5. See Christopher Hitchens, "The Case for Regime Change," in *A Matter of Principle: Humanitarian Arguments for War in Iraq*, ed. Thomas Cushman (Los Angeles: University of California Press, 2005), 31–33.

6. See "The Religious Dimensions of the Torture Debate," Pew Forum on Religion and Public Life, http://pewforum.org/Politics-and-Elections/The-Religious-Dimensions-of-the-Torture-Debate.aspx. For the follow-up story, see "The Torture Debate: A Closer Look," The Pew Forum on Religion and Public Life, http://pewforum.org/Politics-and-Elections/The-Torture-Debate-A-Closer-Look.aspx.

7. Corcoran, *Bitter Harvest*, 5–6, 205–6.

8. Dee Brown, *Bury My Heart at Wounded Knee: An Indian History of the American West* (New York: Holt, Rinehart & Winston, 1970), xxiii.

9. I think we can celebrate this even if we might want to critique Western notions of "rights."

10. Dallas A. Blanchard and Terry J. Prewitt, *Religious Violence and Abortion: The Gideon Project* (Gainesville: University Press of Florida, 1993), ix–xiii, 63–64.

11. See Paul Hill, "I Shot an Abortionist—Short Version," also titled, "Defending the Defenseless," at www.armyofgod.com/PHill_ShortShot.html; also see Dan Clanton, "Biblical Interpretation and Christian Domestic Terrorism: The Exegeses of Rev. Michael Bray and Rev. Paul Hill," *SBL Forum*, http://sbl-site.org/Article.aspx?ArticleID=788.

12. Cited in display at National Memorial, Title II U.S. Code, Section 265F(d). See also The National Counterterrorism Center, "Terrorism Definitions: as of 27 August 2009," www.nctc.gov/site/other/definitions.html.

13. Timothy McVeigh, "Essay on Hypocrisy," distributed by Media Bypass/Alternative Media, Inc., www.outpost-of-freedom.com/mcveigh/okcaug98.htm. I say "attributed to Timothy McVeigh" because I have not been able to confirm authorship apart from finding online sources, some of which dispute that McVeigh wrote the essay. But the incisive question remains attributed to McVeigh.

14. Andrew Bacevich, *The Limits of Power: The End of American Exceptionalism* (New York: Metropolitan Books, 2008). Bacevich was writing prior to the election of Barack Obama. Listen to an interview of Bacevich on the book at www.TokensShow.com/interviews.

Chapter 17 On the Sign of Jonah, and the "Clash of Civilizations" Thesis

1. Mark A. Gabriel, *Culture Clash: Islam's War on the West* (Lake Mary, FL: FrontLine, 2007), 176. Gabriel makes other comments that are simply wrongheaded: "What makes Islam different than all other major religions of the world? Muhammad turned faith into a culture. In other words, when you look at the Muslim world, you will see that Islam is the culture, and the culture is Islam" (1). "To put it more succinctly, religion is the relationship between God and man, and culture is the relationship of man to man" (4). Gabriel is only demonstrating that he is a fundamentalist modernist. As is increasingly understood as we come out from underneath the pall of modernity, faith is inseparable from some cultural expression. Gabriel's "culture clash" is ill argued at its most basic level.

2. Ibid., 176.

3. Rodney Clapp, *A Peculiar People: The Church as Culture in a Post-Christian Society* (Downers Grove, IL: InterVarsity Press, 1996), 155.

4. It is most unfortunate that one of the most popular books in the United States in the last sixty years has been H. Richard Niebuhr's book *Christ and Culture*, which perpetuates a monolithic notion of "culture"—as something that is rejected, accepted, or transformed— as a whole. While numerous critiques have been made, this way of thinking remains profoundly widespread in both "liberal" and "conservative" circles in American Christianity.

5. As Talal Asad, *On Suicide Bombing* (New York: Columbia University Press), 12, puts it: "In brief, there is no such thing as a clash of civilizations because there are no self-contained societies to which fixed civilizational values correspond."

6. Ibid., 9.

7. Ibid.

Chapter 18 On Muslim Hospitality

1. Snjezana Akpinar, "Hospitality in Islam," *Religion East & West* 7 (October 1, 2007): 23.

2. The "Sufis" are a sect of Islam who reject the material order. While this very rejection can and has been critiqued on numerous levels, what is attractive about it is the question that, so far as I can tell, drives it: the question of whether the life of faith is ultimately self-serving or for the sake of one's love of God.

3. St. Hilary of Poitiers, *Contra Constantium imperatorem* 5, cited in Christopher Dawson, *The Making of Europe: An Introduction to the History of the European Unity* (1932; repr., New York: Meridian Books, 1956), 54–55.

4. Sari Nusseibeh with Anthony David, *Once upon a Country: A Palestinian Life* (New York: Farrar, Straus and Giroux, 2007). I have posted an unedited interview I did with Prof. Nusseibeh at www.LeeCCamp.com.

5. Ibid., 12.

6. Ibid., 66.

7. Ibid., 65.

8. Ibid., 66.

9. Ibid., 113.

10. Ibid., 114.

11. Ibid., 115.

12. Ibid., 146.

13. Ibid., 179–80.

Chapter 19 Good Friday

1. See Fr. Rafiq Khoury and Dr. Mustafa Abu Sway, *Jesus: In the Christian and Muslim Faiths* (Jerusalem: Palestinian Academic Society for the Study of International Affairs, 2007), 43–44, where Mustafa Abu Sway responds to this assumed objection in his discussion of the crucifixion of Jesus, noting that for Muslims, repentance for sin—and thus restored relationship with God—remains a simple possibility for believers apart from any such atoning event.

2. There are undoubtedly substitutionary elements much earlier than Calvin. Anselm in the eleventh century popularized the idea of substitution, but for Anselm the substitution was not that of *punishment* but that of *penance*. That is, we needed to make some act of penitential restoration of the honor of God but could not do so: thus the God-man came and freely made such satisfaction on our behalf. But Anselm forthrightly rejected the idea of *punishment*, which Calvin would later popularize. See Anselm of Canterbury, "Why God Became Man," in *Anselm of Canterbury: The Major Works*, ed. Brian Davies and G. R. Evans (Oxford: Oxford University Press, 1998). For an interesting, if perhaps sometimes overstated, discussion of the manner in which Calvin's and, earlier, Anselm's understanding of the doctrine of atonement were both influenced by and influenced their contemporary social practices, see Timothy Gorringe, *God's Just Vengeance: Crime, Violence, and the Rhetoric of Salvation* (New York: Cambridge University Press, 1996).

3. Gustaf Aulén, *Christus Victor: An Historical Study of the Three Main Types of the Idea of Atonement*, trans. A. G. Hebert (1931; repr. Eugene: OR, Wipf and Stock, 2003); Joel B. Green and Mark D. Baker, *Recovering the Scandal of the Cross: Atonement in New Testament and Contemporary Contexts* (Downers Grove, IL: InterVarsity Press, 2000); and Mark D. Baker, ed., *Proclaiming the Scandal of the Cross: Contemporary Images of the Atonement* (Grand Rapids: Baker Academic, 2006).

4. John Howard Yoder, *The Politics of Jesus: Vicit Agnus Noster*, 2nd ed. (Grand Rapids: Eerdmans, 1994), 51.

5. For a classic illustration of this approach, see P. T. Forsyth, *The Justification of God: Lectures for War-Time on a Christian Theodicy* (1917; repr., Eugene, OR: Wipf and Stock, 1999).

6. Jürgen Moltmann, *The Crucified God: The Cross of Christ as the Foundation and Criticism of Christian Theology* (New York: Harper & Row, 1974), 278.

7. I am indebted to my friend David Dark for this phrase.

Chapter 20 The Arab Barbershop, Changing Neighborhoods, and Other Small Exercises in Courage

1. Glen Harold Stassen. "Harry Truman as Baptist President," *Baptist History and Heritage* 34, no. 3 (June 1, 1999): 85. "All of this suggests an interesting thought experiment, part historical and part imagination: if Harry Truman's Baptist heritage had taught him more effectively the practices of peacemaking, how might history have been different. . . . Suppose Harry Truman's church had taught him the absolute rule of just war theory that you must not intentionally target noncombatants, and certainly not bomb cities with mass-destruction weapons like the atomic bomb? Suppose his commitment to doing what is right, combined with specific church teaching, had led him to say, as General Dwight Eisenhower said at the time, that we must not drop atomic bombs on cities. Suppose this had led him to ask for alternatives" (84–85).

Index

Lee C. Camp (PhD, University of Notre Dame) is Professor of Theology and Ethics at Lipscomb University in Nashville, Tennessee. For more information, including audio, video, and other resources, visit LeeCCamp.com. Lee is also the host and creator of Tokens, online at TokensShow.com.